WAITRESS

a memoir

Crystal,

Angel Woolery

Enjoy!

Angel Woolery

Editor: Courtenay Dodds www.courtenaydodds.com

Printed in the United States of America.

ISBN: 0692415394
ISBN-13: 978-0692415399

Preface

Waitress is a collection of anecdotes and random thoughts gathered over the last 30 years or so in my service industry career. I have worked in clubs, bowling alleys, family restaurants and even a semi-fancy place once. As you can imagine, I've seen and heard plenty of weird, gross and funny things, like Penis Man and creamer dish thieves. I can't keep these things to myself. It wouldn't be right. I share my work stories with my friends, who, entertained by the odd behaviour of their fellow humans, told me that I should write a book. Well, here it is.

Contents

Acknowledgments

My handsome husband gets my wholehearted appreciation for more than 20 years of daily foot, neck, leg, head, arm, hand, earlobe, butt cheek and/or back rubs he has given me. Every day he massages away some weird waitress pain. He is so damn wonderful. Without him, I would have given up on this profession years ago because it hurts every muscle in my body at some point during the week.

My undying love and devotion goes to my family and friends for their absolute support of my writing, indeed, their cheerleading for everything I undertake. I am a lucky girl to be surrounded by nothing but awesomeness!

Special thank you to my wonderful mom for letting me use her restaurant as the location for my book cover photo shoot, to Micah of MicahJT Photos for his mad photography skills, and the beautiful Lorie for the lovely prop arrangement.

Thank you so much to my magnificent coworkers for encouraging my frolicsome nature. You make my workdays fly by with all the laughs.

Finally, thank you to the 30 years of customers who have given me enough content to write a book.

Introduction

When I get pedicures, I choose the same color nail polish every time. It's called, 'I'm Not Really a Waitress' by OPI. I don't know if I am in denial or if it's just a pretty shade, but it makes me smile. It also gives me hope of escape. Don't get me wrong, I love waitressing most days, but I didn't think I'd still be doing it well into my 40's. That's damned old for waitresses, strippers and runway models, and I gave up on the two latter professions years ago.

At least a couple of times a week for the last 3 or 4 years, I wake up for work in the morning and think how completely stupid it is that I am still punching a clock. I mean, barring being independently wealthy which would be my first choice, I always fancied I'd get a "real job" at some point. Some point about 20 years ago. I don't exactly know what a "real job" would be but I thought it might involve being salaried and paid vacation time, perhaps with a desk, a computer and a secretary.

I do know that I would like a job where I can pee when I need to instead of holding it in for hours. That can't be healthy. Sick days would be pretty sweet too. I know it's wrong to show up to work all germy and contaminated, but if I need to make the mortgage payment, that's how it's going to have to be. I fantasize about not having to wear a nametag or secure my hair so it doesn't drag through someone's whip cream covered waffle. A "real job" wouldn't physically overwork my poor little body 'til I limp when I walk and wouldn't even think of opening on a holiday. Holidays are for family, friends and sleeping in late. I wish people would stay home and make it unprofitable to even open the doors of any non-essential buildings.

I understand there are travelers and lonely people who need food. I am not heartless. Gas stations should stay open. They have both food and microwaves. I just don't want to work at a place that requires my presence on Christmas Eve or Day, Thanksgiving, Easter, New Year's Eve, New Year's Day, Halloween night, July 4th or Mother's Day. Especially Mother's Day. It is my least favorite day to work. I would rather live off canned meat and curdled strawberry milk in a tent under a bridge along the Cuyahoga River before subjecting myself to it ever again.

So, why do I still labor away like a peasant? Mostly because I am poor if I don't work. It's decent money and I don't suck at it. I love my co-workers and I don't yet know what I want to be when I grow up. I could be or do anything but I am dragging my ass because what I really want is to create art and write words.

I love words and I love to talk. Waitressing is a profession that allows me to do that ALL DAY LONG. So I waitress, and I complain about it, and I'll keep going back for more. Unless this book sees me banned from the service industry for all eternity. I'd be real torn up about that. Not.

1

I Am Little, But I Will Kick Your Ass

At an impressive 5 feet tall, I couldn't appear mean or dangerous even if I tried. I almost always smile, even when there's nothing to smile about and when I am angry, I smile real hard.

I can get riled easily though and when I do, I feel kind of fighty. It's probably all those pent up waitress emotions struggling to escape. I've squashed those suckers down for too many years and they are starting to resist. So far, I've managed to not throw a single punch, but that's only because I'm ridiculously nice. Someday, when I crack, I'm hoping that someone photo documents it so that I can savor the spectacle at my leisure.

Restaurantal expectations should gradually heighten the higher the tab is. For a $200.00 meal and a $40-50 dollar tip, you may snap your fingers once or twice at the help. You will still be taking your life in your hands by doing so, make no mistake. For a $4.99 plate of ass widening pancakes and a glass of water, you would do well to say please and thank you, because the girl delivering that pile of hot syrupy goodness could be ready to snap.

Front of the house employees as a rule are hyper-social people. One could not do the job were that not the case. I do believe however that over time, patience begins to wear thin. Stupidity melts one's glossy, outer layer of happiness like a flamethrower would a block of processed cheese. Then, only innate civility reins in impolite reactions, and possibly some tiny glowing ember of lingering love for humanity. This is where I often find myself.

~~~~~

I was taking an order from 3 teenaged girls at Table #35 when a regular decided to massage my shoulders on his way out. He rubbed for about 30 seconds before my lack of acknowledgment encouraged him to stop, or maybe my tense waitress muscles just tired his hands. I don't know, but that's not the point. I wouldn't even let my husband rub my shoulders while I was at a table and I do enjoy me some shoulder rubs.

#awkward #rubharder #donotouchthewaitress

~~~

I would like to thank Table #22 for speaking slowly and enunciating the word 'lemon' so that I could successfully get her 'l e m o n' into her diet pop.

~~~

Sit where you're told and no one gets hurt.

Sure! The hostess will smile and let you sit where you want after you turn your nose up at her seating suggestion. It's not like there's a system in place or anything that you are completely fucking up by going all rogue and shit. You just caused the hostess to get yelled at by a waitress, you heartless bastard.

~~~

If I arrive at a table to do my job, why don't customers stop talking and acknowledge my presence? Is it really a surprise that I need to talk to them?

~~~

If you do not know what you want to order, please don't lie and tell your waitress that you do and then sit discussing what you want to order with your friend. That might be the day your waitress is ready to snap.

~~~

While working the graveyard shift, a catfight broke out between two drunken female guests. During the course of their slapping, screaming, and ripping out of hair extensions, they dragged their mayhem through the entire restaurant. The cops had to break it up.

When the morning manager came in and found out about the altercation, he suspiciously eyed my wrist brace and asked, "What did you do last night?!"

~~~

I get a nearly overwhelming urge to run down the aisles at work holding menus in each hand, arms extended, making the clickety clack sound on people's heads like cards on bicycle spokes.

~~~

A smart assed teenage boy at Table #14 called me Flo.

I placed my hands on the table, leaned a little closer and said, "I want to let you know that I am the last person to touch your food before you get it." Then I stood back up, prepared my pen and ticket book to take their order and smiled sweetly.

*Flo is a character from a late 70's, early 80's TV show called Alice. Google it. It's worth the 5 seconds it will take.

~~~

I have your pie right here. \ /

~~~

I had a regular tell me he was going to leave my tip at the cash register. He was adamant that I make sure I got the money, and if he hadn't been, I'd have never known what I do now.

This customer always tipped $4.00, so I checked every few minutes for the tip receipt to print out on our pantry printer. After about 15 minutes of nothing and asking the hostess about it repeatedly, I had someone with a higher level of POS access check for me. (POS meaning Point of Sale, not Piece of Shit.) The hostess had not sent it through, despite her many assurances to the contrary. She told me she had been doing it the same way for a year. Wrongly. Which meant, not at all.

If she had not been entering the tips and still collecting the money, the register would have been over by many, many dollars at the end of each day and a red flag would have been raised a year before when she started. Effectively she was sticking her hand in my apron and taking money out of my pocket. If I were inclined to give her the benefit of doubt, believing she were simply stupid and doing it wrong, that would mean at least half the staff have been shorted hundreds of dollars over the course of the last year. I could have throttled her.

I found myself very angry and in the middle of the lunch rush when she came up to apologize. I told her that I didn't want to talk because I was supremely pissed off at her and we could discuss it later. She would not drop it. I spoke a little more strongly. She called me a bitch.

Me, the victim of her heartless crime. I thought my f-
bombs were quietly hitting her in the face until my General
Manager (whom I love so much by the way) came tearing into
the pantry to scold us like naughty little girls and then sent us
very firmly in opposite directions.

No official action was ever taken against that tip-stealing
bitch. No write up. No stern talking to. Nothing. I shanked
that wretched ho in dry storage after the lunch rush was over.
She bled out amidst the oatmeal and sugar packets.

(Only in the dry storage of my mind, of course.)

~~~

I think the guy at Table #53 is making fun of my chipper
demeanour. Not nice Table #53.

Not nice.

~~~

Me: Holding a tray that is too heavy for my tray arm alone,
I lean way back, limbo style, to better balance as I place the
items on the table.

The elderly lady at Table #63 says, "It's a good thing you
got that big belly to rest it on."

She's lucky she's cute.

~~~

It's a long, stupid story but we don't cut our toast at work.
We just don't.

Table #35 says, completely serious, "Darn it Angel! You forgot to cut my toast."

(He knows we don't cut it and he didn't ask.)

Me: "Would you like me to cut your toast for you?"

Table #35: "Yes please."

#ffs #youhaveaknife #coddledmuch?

~~~

My section at work was a sea of slow talking and indecision today. As I stood wearing my patient face for the umpteenth time, my mind wandered. I began to fantasize about turning into a tiny, rabid monkey and springing upon an unsuspecting head or two in an attempt to coax forth an order so that I could maybe serve the 20 other people waiting for my mad skillz.

~~~

The next customer that exclaims "Oh! There you are!" is getting an angry, quick little-fisted throat punch while I smile sweetly at them.

~~~

I went to clear off a few tables and grab my tips only to find that they were all gone. I looked around and saw that a new guy had joined his friends at Table #19. I held my hand out in front of him and barked, "Give me my money back right now!"

He sheepishly reached in his pocket and handed me back all the money to the accompaniment of his friends saying, "Ooooo you're busted!" "She got you!"

A complete shithead with shithead friends. I suspect they will go far in life. Not.

~~~

Table #60 pointed at a picture of fruit and asked, "Is this oatmeal?"

Me: (In my mind) "Um. No. It's fruit."

Wtf?

Then, in my mind, I slapped her repeatedly.

~~~

If I assault someone with the business end of a crayon and they do not die, is it considered a deadly weapon?

~~~

Someone complained to corporate that I was rude. It made me giggle all day. I know who they were. I should have been rude.

Me: "Clearly they're liars."

My manager: "Yeah, you were rude. The one who can't stop smiling."

:) It's nice to be impervious to lies.

They made several alterations to the ingredients listed on the menu items they ordered, adding some and taking others away. I accommodated. Most importantly, the cooks accommodated. When I delivered the food, one of the women said her meal was cold. I had it remade and redelivered the food. She said it was wrong. I offered to have it remade again and she got pissy, said no and started picking at it like a petulant 3 year old. So, I sent the manager over to talk to her and she ended up getting her meal free. She then ate all of it. I guess free food must taste better.

Then, she called our corporate office and complained. Maybe she did not care for my professional demeanour in the face of her ridiculous attitude and instead I should have groveled a little. That will never, ever happen.

I have a low opinion of people who call the corporate office of a business to complain about petty shit. They obviously don't have enough to keep them entertained in their sad little lives. I have an exceedingly low opinion of people who call the corporate office of a business to complain about imaginary things that their own crazy ass invented. But the lowest opinion I hold in this area rests on the corporate offices who kowtow to this obnoxious behaviour thus encouraging it to continue. Just the thought of our society's inflated sense of self-entitlement makes me feel downright revolutionary. I may rise up and wrest control back single-handedly.

~~~

It's obvious many other waitresses have screwed up your weird order Table #72 lady.

Even though it was not me who did such a thing, I understand your distress. Truly, I do. It would be super nice however if, while you were enunciating your special requests, you wouldn't talk so loudly that my ears want to bleed. I hear you woman. Clearly. And so do ALL the other customers in the restaurant.

~~~

Me: "Hello. My name is Angel. I will be your server."

Table #10: "Is that your real name or your stage name?"

Me: "I will not be dancing today."

~~~

The next customer who mocks my chipper demeanour is going to get cold cocked with the business end of my serving tray.

~~~

I wish I could meet whoever invented the 5-day workweek so I could kick their ass.

~~~

Ordering food is not freakin' rocket science Table #65 man. Bacon and eggs need not take 5 minutes to relay to me. Some day that fantasy about whacking people upside the head with my ticket book will come to pass. Perhaps today.

~~~

An impatient young couple decided to not wait for the hostess to seat them while we were busy. I saw them headed toward my section so I grabbed a couple of menus and was right behind them. They didn't see me. As the guy rounded Table #34, he reached out, scooped up my tip that was sitting on the edge, stuck it in his pocket and sat down. Motherfucker. I held out my hand and loudly told him to give me my damn tip back. He complied immediately, probably because I'm scary. Then I went up to the cops we had on duty in the lobby and had them escort him and his date out of the restaurant.

Ladies, if your man steals tips, dump his ass. In fact, if you're on a date and your man tips less than 20%, dump his ass. He is a cheapskate and you can do way better. Trust me.

~~~

FYI Table #13 lady, if you are still deciding what to have, YOU ARE NOT READY TO ORDER.

Your waitress is oft times working at a speed you cannot begin to fathom. That lie you told is costing her precious moments. Moments in which she could deliver food to a table before it gets cold or refill a drink before a customer is forced to make obnoxious slurping sounds in their empty glass. Maybe just enough moments that she can actually go pee. I am sure my bladder is stretched out and thinned like an overstuffed trash bag on moving day. I hold it in for hours praying for those scarce 60 seconds of opportunity to let it out. If you say you are ready to order when I am busy and then hem and haw over 3 different pages of the menu, fuck you. I am walking away. It is the safest course of action for both of us.

*****

Angel Woolery

2

Quit Playing With It
and Just Eat It
and Other Weird Food Stuff

It's not foreplay people. It's lunch. In a restaurant. In public. Know your food. Respect your food. Maintain your dignity.

In an attempt at fairness, I will list a few of my weird food habits:

- I'll lick my plate if it was tasty enough. Wherever, whenever.

- I eat the edges of peanut butter cups and the center of my malted milk balls first.

- I eat ketchup on my bacon.

- I only like to eat the yolks of eggs.

- I dislike it when the bartender hand squeezes lime into my vodka. I will drink it, but still...

- I will eat the top of a muffin and leave the rest.

- I require a side cup of syrup so I can dip my butterless pancakes.

- Raw sugar, organic sugar or no sugar and I'm relentless about it.

- I only enjoy the ends of sausage links.

- The middle piece of bread in a club sandwich makes me irate and I will rip it out in frustration.

- If I am dining on particularly delicious food, I make happy noises while I eat.

However, we are not talking about me, and it's way funnier when you get to see everyone else's weirdness in action.

~~~~~

Table #33 cut their pancake into eight, mostly even, pie-like wedges and only ate two of them.

~~~

Table #64 drank 4 huge glasses of pop. Is he reconstituting himself or getting every penny's worth?

~~~

The woman at Table #76 is eating her leftover salad dressing out of the ramekin with her fingers.

~~~

Every time Table #35 comes in and orders Pecan Pie, she tells me to make it hotter than the last time. That pie was boiling when I brought it. You could see it moving up and down almost as if it were breathing. I warned her to be careful when I set it down. Her adult son looked freaked out and told her it was too hot. She told him that was how she wanted it and took a bite.

Perfection.

~~~

Me: How would you like your egg?

Table #73: Sunny side up, but not too runny.

~~~

Table #13 goobed a good six inch trail of gravy down his shirt and without any hesitation, grabbed his spoon, reversed the trail in a skillful scoop and ate the shirt gravy.

~~~

Table #64 woman had a bowl of chili with cheese, cornbread, french fries and a grilled cheese with bacon, all while not in any way acknowledging the Weight Watcher's book she brought with her that sat to her left.

#myhero

~~~

The girls at Table #25 made lemonade out of the water, lemon wedges and sugar packets.

My husband and I were out to eat at a rib joint and a table of 6 middle aged women next to us were making lemonade with wild abandon. Seriously, you'd think they were at a lemonade making party. Squeezing those wedges without even bothering to look sheepish about it. I noticed right away because my waitress senses were sparking furiously. After a while, my husband looked over. He leans in and says to me incredulously, "They're making lemonade!!"

Yep.

This happens often. It's extremely tacky.

Lemonade makers are a damned blight upon decent society. If I had my way, I'd charge them for a side of fruit and smack them upside the head.

Don't be a lemonade maker.

~~~

Table #54 put a generous amount of ketchup in his chili.

I do not have such a sophisticated palate.

~~~

I am sorry Table #61, but company policy does not allow for the return of your salad because you are too full now.

~~~

I have no idea how many people I've seen devour a packet of jelly.

#patiencehungrydiners #yourfoodiscooking

~~~

Table #63, a teenaged girl, added artificial sweetener to her pop. How freakin' revolting?! I almost knocked her glass off the table and scolded her for her disgusting behaviour.

Instead, I shoved all that emotion deep down in order to have it burst forth to share with you after I clocked out.

~~~

Table #60 ordered 2 hot waters and asked for a dish of creamers. It seems they brought their own "special" tea. Their words, not mine.

(One of the tea bags was the exact same stuff we serve. The other was the same flavor, different brand.) They later waved me over to get them a coffee urn full of hot water for their stupid, "special" tea.

Some people order tea, pay for the tea, but use their own. This is admirable and I approve.

However, if a customer brings their own tea and pays nothing, I expect them to bring creamer, lemon, honey, and any of the other things they require to make their tea palatable instead of asking me for it. Come to think of it, they can bring their own hot water too.

~~~

I'm sorry nice Table #25 lady. I cannot make your toast darker because it already has butter on it. You have to wait for completely new toast.

~~~

Table #64 ate the guts out of her muffin. The entire outside is still sitting there.

#madmuffinskillz

~~~

Table #62 flags me over to show me the two pieces of bone that he found in his bone-in ham slice.

It's times like this that I stand slack jawed and frozen. My breath coming in fast, anxious little puffs as I struggle fiercely to slap that filter in place before the words can leap free.

~~~

Table #75 woman is dipping her buttered, peanut buttered, English muffin into her whipped cream topped hot chocolate.

~~~

Table #63 pointed to a picture of sunny side up eggs and asked me if they were hard.

I said no, this is hard and I thunked him firmly in the forehead with my +7 Pen of Correction. (In my mind)

* +7 is a reference to a game called Dungeons and Dragons. You roll the dice to enhance weapons or special skills. If you roll a 7 on something, it would then be a +7 something, either delivering that much damage or having that much extra oomph.

~~~

Table #72 put mustard in their chili.

~~~

Table #31 ate ketchup off his filthy, stained, not washed in a decade winter coat, with his hand.

~~~

Table #34 orders her 2 pieces of bacon "so well done that it breaks".

I bring the bacon.

Table #34 gestures to the first and pokes at the second respectively. "This piece needs to be cooked longer and I don't know what's wrong with this piece."

Me, speaking of the second one: "That piece broke when we were putting it on the plate."

Table #34: "It looks weird. It's in pieces."

Me: "You look weird."

Hahaha! Ok no, I didn't say that. I got her an unbroken piece of bacon. Seriously though, people are challenged.

Angel Woolery

*****

3

Dumb. Dumb. Dumb.

Did your mother ever tell you, "Quit making that face or it will freeze like that!"? Mine did. It turns out that she was right. Mine is frozen in a look of judgment, with a crease where the skin above my right eyebrow lifts and squinches repeatedly, softened by a service industry smile second to none.

~~~~~

Me: "Can I bring you coffee or perhaps iced tea to start you off?"

Table #72: 3 people order coffee and the 4th person says, "It's too cold for iced tea. I'll have water."

~~~

The stuff in the pink packets is aspartame, or, as I like to call it, sweet death. It is not pink sugar. Stop calling it that immediately.

~~~

Table #67

Woman #1: "I heard they're making Fifty Shades of Grey into a movie."

Woman #2: "Well, I don't like that idea at all!"

Me (in my mind, where no one could hear): *Why the hell wouldn't that be a good idea?? Are you feeling all right?*

~~~

The 3 boys at Table #33 are stoned out of their minds. Coloring.

~~~

Table #60 man: "I'll have my eggs sunny side easy."

Me: "I don't know what you're talking about. Up like this picture or flipped over...over easy?"

Table #60 man: "Over easy."

I brought him over easy and when I checked back, he was poking at his eggs and pouting.

Table #60 woman: "He can't eat those. They're runny."

Me: "That is how he ordered them."

Table #60 woman: "He doesn't like them runny."

The guy knows he's wrong and keeps saying he doesn't need anything and that he will keep the eggs.

Me: "Does he like no runniness? Because that is called over hard. I will have them remade."

I had them remade and sent the manager out. She comped their whole check to save herself the frustration idiocy causes.

I stopped back to find out if all was well.

Table #60 woman hands me $5 and says: "I want you to have this. It's not your fault the cooks don't know how to make eggs."

~~~

The American guy at Table #33 asked me what applesauce is.

~~~

The uncouth woman at Table #23 has been sitting for about an hour (even before her food was ordered) with her large paper napkin spread fully open across her generous bosom.

~~~

It's super busy and the guy at Table #75 keeps stopping me. "Waitress!" "Waitress?"

"Can you get me ...." " Oh waitress! I need..." Over and over and over. He keeps stopping me and I keep getting his stuff. But I am very busy, AND I am not his damn waitress. His waitress is about a foot taller than me and has much darker hair. I finally can't take it anymore so I loudly say to him, "Look at me! Look at my face! I. Am. Not. Your. Waitress."

Table #75 says, "Oh. You all look the same."

~~~

Table #24 lady was giving me a hard time from the moment she sat down. I smiled sweetly through all of it. I'll skip the part where she insists broccoli soup should have wild rice in it and the part involving our lack of fancy coffee and flavored cream and go right to my two favorites.

Side note to clarify: For some dumbass reason we are no longer allowed to bring crackers with soup if there is bread on the plate, unless they are requested. I won't even touch our lame butter rules.

I deliver her soup with bread.

Lady: "What? I don't get crackers?" She looks at me like I'm a fucking simpleton who doesn't know crackers come with soup.

Me, feeling a tad snarky: "I am sorry, our corporate policy forbids me to bring crackers with bread unless it is requested. I will get you some."

Lady: "No. That's fine."

Me: "No, really. I can bring them as long as you requested them."

Lady: "No. That's ok. I don't like the crackers here."

Sigh.

Later...

Lady: "Do your pie apples really come from China?"

Me: "Uhm. No. I doubt it."

Lady: "Then why does it say on your dessert menu that most apples are produced in China?"

Me: "There are interesting facts throughout the dessert menu. The Chocolate Pie says something about chocolate being for love. I am hoping they don't expect love to break out in the restaurant."

~~~

I gave Table #52 a head tilt WITH two raised eyebrows. Oops. It's getting harder to hide the riptide of waitress emotions.

~~~

Table #54: "Will the sun shine through the windows and get us?"

Me: "I don't know. It depends if the clouds move."

~~~

A young, good looking couple sat at Table #33. I overhear the guy say to the girl: "Edible panties? I don't think I like that idea."

I am surprised his darn pants did not light on fire.

#liarliar

~~~

The woman at Table #54 waved her coupons at me and asked if she can use them.

Me, after looking: "No. They expired last month."

Her: "I don't understand. The ones on the other side aren't expired."

Me, after looking again: "Those are for a different restaurant."

Her: "But I don't understand. I should be able to use them."

Me: "They are for a different restaurant."

Her: "But they are not expired. I don't understand why these are."

Me: OMFG. I internalize the eye roll and have a fantasy of vigorously smacking her upside her head. "Those are for a sandwich shop. Different restaurants make different expiration dates."

Her: "So I can't use them?"

WTF.

~~~

I rubbed my face in exasperation while standing at Table #34 today as an extremely audible sigh escaped me. Waitressing is taxing at times.

~~~

How hard is it to find your food hole with your fork Table #53? Poke until you no longer encounter resistance. Don't give up and let it fall to the floor.

~~~

Table #35: The woman on the left orders a pop and then immediately changes her mind and orders water. The woman on the right orders a diet pop.

Woman on the left: "After what I saw on the news the other night, I cannot bring myself to get a pop."

Woman on the right: "What did you see?"

Woman on the left: "Scientists say that it can give you Diabetes."

Woman on the right: *some mumbled acknowledgment*

Woman on the left: "But that's just in lab rats so far. So we're fine."

FACEPALM

*****

4

Cutie Patooties

These are the people that make my workday interesting and pleasant. They are lovely customers who invite kindness with their wonderful attitudes and polite manners. My favorites however, are the older people carrying around a hint of devilry or a haphazard approach to dressing themselves. One older lady still sticks fondly in my memory because she had buttoned her long spring jacket horribly crooked and she had a happy, vacant look residing upon her sweet face. I hope that if I am ever ancient and have lost some of my mental faculties, that I look wonderfully unconcerned and cheerful. And drunk. It never hurts to look a little drunk when you're old.

~~~~~

Table #25 is easily 90 years old. Her wig is the lushest, most glorious mass of butt length platinum blonde tresses you'd ever want to see adorn a pretty little head. Should I ever find myself in need of covering a balding noggin that is the one I am getting.

~~~

Table #34 man: "We can't forget your name. You're The Angel."

~~~

Table #60 lady starts unbuttoning her shirt, gets 3 or 4 buttons down and giggles. She says, "Oh! I thought I had a shirt on under here. I guess I don't." Re-buttons.

~~~

Table #41 was in celebrating her upcoming 107th birthday.

I asked her if she wanted coffee.

She says, "Coffee? No. Do you have any booze in your car?"

~~~

I was done taking Table #52's order and turned to walk away.

Table #52 guy: "Angel?"

Me: "Yes?"

Table #52 guy: "Nothing. I just wanted to say your name."

Ha! Funny guy!

~~~

I waited on Brian Kelley from Florida Georgia Line and one of his production guys today. They were darlings and kept calling me honey and sweetie. I love that! It struck me as funny that the production guy was wearing flip flops. Because of this and my friend Christian, I believe this may be an industry standard.

Christian is a dear friend and a fabulous dancer. He also produces the live video content for the Broadway smash: Rain - A Tribute to the Beatles. (Go see it, it's awesome!) I have never seen his cute tootsies in anything but flip flops. Ever.

~~~

Table #72 asked his friend, "In which state of the union did you live in the longest?"

~~~

Table #60 is verbally mapping out for me the route he will drive from his hotel, which he got a great deal on, to the Polka Festival next weekend in Ohio.

~~~

My little old German lady at Table #40 told me I was a naughty, naughty girl and she'd have to spank me.

She makes me happy.

~~~

A table of old people were telling me how to divide the checks. One gestures to two others and says, "We're a threesome." and giggles.

~~~

Table #52 told me I was strong for such a little thing.

~~~

I was explaining to my cutie old lady regulars (who must be 80ish) that I was dressing up as a Hello Kitty zombie girl for my husband's band, 'The Tone Zombie's' Halloween show this weekend and that I may be too old for this sort of thing. They assured me that I was never too old. They told me that one of the ladies dressed up as a pirate the previous week and her other friend, a witch. Apparently, she did too many jag and cherry bombs and was quite hung-over at church the next day. I love them so much!!

*****

5

Rude Fuckers

These are the ones that speak down to you, make ridiculous demands and complain about petty crap. They take up your time with needy drama and have no regard for the feelings of those around them. You know these people. You may even have the pleasure of working with them or for them. You might even be related to one of them. Thankfully, I don't have to wait on them too often because I'd have been fired or incarcerated by now. It is rare that they direct their attitude in my personal direction but it does happen, and I possess less restraint with each incident. This kind of behaviour would get you kicked out of a place 20 years ago. Now, corporate restaurants at least, cave to the asshats and their douchebaggery is rewarded with a free meal. Screw that. I say we treat them the way we use to. Like social pariahs, unfit for polite society, where they learn to treat others with a little respect or they are left to suffer a lonely, horrible existence.

~~~~~

I walked by the drunk guy at Table #1 and see that he has unscrewed the salt shaker top and he is spitting his pop into it. Gross. I tossed a straw on the table from out of my apron pocket and told him to dig the wet salt out of the narrow shaker. I went about my business expecting compliance. A few minutes later, I looked over and he was gone. I spied him in the lobby by the door and his friend was paying the tab. I walked over to him, took his arm, walked him back to the table, and repeated the instructions. "Clean out the shaker." Then I sat at the table across from him and supervised until he'd done an acceptable job.

Asshole.

~~~

My eye is starting to twitch, compliments of the cranky bitch at Table #53. Now, I don't like to break out the "B" word, but truly, it is appropriate.

~~~

Table #54 is too hungry to wait for the girl with him to order and has me cooking his food without her order in. He didn't even give her time to decide.

~~~

Table #66 guy is such a self-entitled buttface, I bet he even googoo'd as a little baby that his momma's teat milk wasn't the right temperature for him and had her hold her boobs over low heat.

~~~

It seems I spoke sternly enough to Table #65 man last time he was in that he remembered not to complain about his imaginary complaints, but not too sternly that he forgot to tip me.

There was a dual effort to piss me off the last time he was in between him and someone completely unrelated: The restaurant was COMPLETELY full except for a few recently vacated tables that needed to be cleared and wiped. The lobby was COMPLETELY full. There was a waiting list and the 3 hostesses and the managers were running their asses off. Every waitress in the building was under immense stress.

I was standing at a table taking an order when some impatient jerkwad from the lobby walked up to me and said in a snarky voice, "Can I get some service?" Why yes fuckhead, you certainly can.

I excused myself from my table with the sweetest of smiles and walked him up to the waitlist and asked, "What's your name and how many?"

Impatiently, the old guy says, "I see empty tables." While trying not to kick his ill-mannered ass, I politely informed him that he would go on the waitlist. That is when the earlier mentioned Table #65 man came up to me and asked how long. I told him 30 minutes and asked for his name.

He said, "I see an empty table right there. Can we have that one?"

I flayed him with my baby blues and calmly, but sternly used my perky waitress voice, "No! It's dirty and there are so many people before you! What's your name? I will put you on the list."

~~~

I am about to do violence to Table #61 man's slow talking, dumb fucking question asking, nothing better to do but hassle the waitress, head. He is deliberately being obtuse just to amuse himself. Jerk.

~~~

I'm waiting on the biggest prick I have ever had the misfortune to wait upon.

I am trying to take a woman's order. Whenever I ask her something, she looks at him. He repeats to her exactly what I have just said. She tells him what she wants and then he tells me. Odd.

At this point, I am speculating whether he is an abusive control freak or some weird sex game has stumbled out into public. What am I supposed to do? Slip her a note under her french fries asking if she needs help? I have no idea. I continue to slowly and painfully extract her order. Then, it's his turn. He tells me that he wants a side of french toast. This is one piece of bread cut in half and he is a big guy, so I need to clarify. I start to ask him the question that will clear it all up and he snaps at me, "Bring me what I ordered, dammit."

So I did. At which point he loses his freakin' mind because it is the wrong amount.

Mid-tirade about how stupid I am, I lean a little closer, throw my arms wide in a gesture of feduppedness and clearly and loudly say, "Oh my god!" right to his stupid face and then walk away.

I never went back. Fuck that guy.

Poor Rose was my supervisor that night. I don't go rogue too often. Lucky her! She was sure we would both end up jobless. I hope over the years that I have made up for the stress I caused her that evening.

~~~

Table #35 answered her stupid phone right in the middle of giving me her order.

No, excuse me.

No apology.

No nothing.

I walked away.

No, excuse me.

No apology.

No nothing.

~~~

Some impatient dickhead walked his ass to the back of a plumb full restaurant to see if there were open tables. He chose to stop me in the middle of the lunch rush to say, "How come I have to be on a waiting list if there are open tables?" (There were two open tables, one was dirty, one was an 8 top.)

First, fuck you. You are not fucking special. I told him as I gestured to a set up party table, "I have a party of 22 coming. That empty booth is my booth and I cannot take any new tables. Go back up front."

~~~

The middle aged man at Table #62 took a huge gamble with his personal safety when he waved my tired, old waitress ass over to tell me that he'd dropped chunks of onion out of his burger and into the aisle and then gestured that I could clean it up for him.

I am quickly nearing the end of my waitress career.

~~~

The ladies at Table #64 have on so much perfume that I can taste it from 6 feet away and smell it from 25. French whores would wear less.

~~~

I think that if that woman has time to flag me down and repeatedly tell me that she dropped a napkin under the table, the same woman might lean her lazy ass over and pick up the napkin she dropped under the table. Just a suggestion.

*****

6

Nice Customers

I want you to know I am actually a nice, competent waitress with only an occasional short fuse. I would say that a majority of the people I wait on are polite. I know they should get more attention but the buttheads are the ones that fuel the conversation in the server aisle most days. So, thank you very much to the nice customers who make this job pleasant. I wish I could wait on you and only you every single day!

~~~~~

A very nice married couple that comes in regularly fixed my brakes, both front and rear for free. I paid for the parts and they did the rest. They saved me hundreds of dollars and quite a lot of stress. They did not hesitate to help me when I needed it and they wanted nothing in return.

The only thing I could think to do was to buy them lunch. Not only are they great customers, they have turned into wonderful friends.

~~~

All of my customers today, every single one, were pleasant, complimentary, mighty fine tippers, flirts or general cutie pies. They laughed at my jokes. They ordered what I suggested. They told me I was wonderful. They said I did a good job. I wish every workday was as perfect as today.

~~~

My winning smile and sunny disposition turned the cranky, muscled guy at Table #30 into a winker. Yay!!

~~~

We tipped our waitress $323.00 tonight. We heard mad giggling from the back of the house. It turns out they all split their tips. Yay!! Happiness!!

I added this story because it is waitress related and it made me very happy. My husband's company gave a group of their employees a gift certificate to a supper club in the middle of nowhere. It was a reward for some great accomplishment. There were about 15-20 people in our group. We ate everything we wanted, drank everything we wanted and when we were done, there was $323.00 dollars left. After a few minutes of discussion, we all decided to give the remainder to the waitress for her tip and ended up making 3 waitresses madly happy.

~~~

Table #63 woman to me: "You're always so wonderful!"

Me: *blush*

Table #63: "It's true. You are."

~~~

Table #34 to me: "Thank you for being our waitress."

I must've been sparkly today.

~~~

I decided that the weird look customers give me right before they give me a big tip is not a weird look at all. It is a look of awe at my mad waitressing skillz.

~~~

I can only conclude from the $14 tip that my 2 top of older ladies left me, that I am amazing at my chosen profession.

~~~

I overheard Table #34 lady say to her friend as I walked away, "We've had her before. She's good."

That's what he said. :)

~~~

I got another $20 tip from the sweeties at Table #24.

#waitressmagicinprogress

~~~

A lady at Table #67 informed me I was "so precious".

That's right bitches. Precious.

~~~

It seems I was dazzling waitress perfection today.

Table #64 man: "Thank you for being our waitress today."

Me: "You're welcome. Thank you for coming in."

sparkles

~~~

Table #51: "You're the best waitress here. We're going to request you every time."

Me: "You're going to make my head big."

Table #51: "You deserve it."

It's ok fellow servers, you're still above average, but I'm the "best". :p

~~~

Sweetie pie little old lady at table #51 reaches her lovely hand to mine and grabs hold and says, "You are sooooooo cute!"

<3 <3 So sweet.

~~~

Table #63 is already looking at me like I'm super weird and I've only brought them drinks and taken their order. I expect that the tip will be humongous.

~~~

Table #54 to me: "You're awesome!"

Me: "Thanks! You can stay all day." :)

*****

Angel Woolery

7

Waitress Nightmares

If you wait tables for any length of time, dreams and nightmares are bound to come crashing unannounced through what would otherwise be a restful night. Some stressful moment will trigger them and then, watch out! Customers you've never seen before will haunt your REM sleep. They will arrive by the busload and you'll have no cook on duty. They will demand things you don't have and you will have to run through a mess of flesh eating mouse lemurs to get to the grocery store so you can get the stuff to fulfill their orders. Your manager will have you scrubbing the yellow lines in the parking lot with a bristleless toothbrush while your tables wait an hour for you to bring them their drinks.

It could take a week for it to start happening. It could take several years. Know that when the dreams begin, it likely signals that it is a good time to change professions. No one does, of course. I sure didn't. But I didn't know then what I do now.

I remember quite clearly the day that started my nighttime disturbances. I was a fresh-faced 18 year old and I'd recently moved from the Midwest to California. I had waitressed in a little family restaurant for a few years that maybe sat 40 people when it was full. I loved it and I had a knack for it, so that was what I decided to do when I moved. The new restaurant I worked in was a little more upscale than I'd been accustomed to and served beer and wine.

I remember being a little weirded out because I had to carry a corkscrew as part of my waitress gear. I don't even think I'd had a glass of wine yet at that point in my life. Soup or salad came with every meal, which really added to the workload, and we also served dessert. I was up for the challenge and I loved it! My mad serving skillz were being polished to a sparkle and the money was making me hungry for more. One day in particular however, I did not love.

It was a lunch shift. Nothing too exciting ever happened at lunch. There was always one cook, the manager and myself on the schedule. We never needed more than that. We had gotten a reservation for a party of 30. No biggy. The head waitress worked across the street at a car dealership and agreed to pop over on her lunch hour to help out.

We had the normal trickle of lunch customers come in. Then, the party of 30 arrived and one man's douchebaggery started while I was still bringing the drinks. A tray in each hand, full of drinks and he's all, "Where's MY drink?" Because I was not yet fed up and worn out from the ridiculous shit people say and do, I did not dump the whole damn setup on his stupid head and walk out the door, leaving them to starve. Instead, I assured him his drink would be in the next set of trays my short little arms were going to bring out so fast, it would seem magic little elves must have poured the drinks for me. Jerk. Then the group started running me for things. Why people cannot place all their requests at one time has always been a mystery to me. It puts me in the weeds* faster than anything.

While this was going on, the rest of the dining room filled up and the head waitress had to go back to her day job. That left a full dining room, one cook, the manager and me. At the end of my shift, I gathered what little strength I had left and went to look at the occupancy sign to see if it were really as bad as it had seemed. It was forever seared into my memory.

Occupancy 156.

I don't know how many seated customers that translated to but it must have been at least one hundred. It felt like way more.

Everyone survived. Most of the customers were very patient. I did not cry, I did not harm anyone and no one left hungry. I have never had another shift even come close to rivaling the mental trauma of that day. That was the week my waitress nightmares started.

*In the weeds: When you're really fucking overwhelmed with customers and just one more thing added to your workload will tip you over the edge of sanity. This often ends in tears and vehemently swearing that you are going find some other line of work because this waitressing crap is bullshit. There are much easier ways to earn a dollar.

~~~~~

I had a stupid waitress dream.

I was getting my ass handed to me with a bunch of new tables that were ordering super slow. I mean sloth slow. I finally got all of their drink orders minus one table's, only to find out that we were out of pop. I grabbed the last glass in the rack and ran to another building to change out the pop boxes. As I was running back clutching the glass, sliding around on a snowy sidewalk in non-skid proof shoes, the manager grabbed hold of me jokingly and would not let me go. Grrrr. I finally get back to find that one of the other girls was getting her pop with no problem and my new table already had their drinks. Freakin' stressful! I woke up worn out. I hate stupid waitress dreams.

~~~

Last night, while I slept, I served my customers coffee while they sat on my bed.

~~~

I had a horrible waitress nightmare last night. Horrible. There was much sobbing and seconds before quitting, I woke up. I'm surprised I wasn't actually crying.

~~~

How can a girl get a restful night's sleep when the hostess goes missing and she, herself is stuck at the cash register watching her section fill up? She can't.

~~~

I just woke up from the middle of a waitress nightmare.

My first thought: Now those customers will never get handled.

My second thought: Some other waitress will fall asleep and arrive in the middle of that dream and complete my work. Or not, depending on her level of stress.

~~~

Why is the pop machine never where it is supposed to be? In last night's dream, it was in the basement. Deep, deep in the basement.

~~~

I had to let my surrounding tables go unacknowledged while I took a party table's order.

In the middle of taking that order, the party table walked down the road to a pub where they wanted to wait while their food was cooking. I had to follow along behind writing on little pieces of paper to complete the order. When I got back to the computer, I couldn't find all the little pieces of paper and started crying. I wanted to quit, but if I did, that would mean that Dora Lee would have to work Christmas Day after requesting it off and I love her too much to do that to her. I woke up crying.

~~~

I had one of those waitress nightmares and woke up with a headache and a bad attitude. I'm going to shake it off and spread joy. In about an hour.

~~~

I had a horrible dream last night that my customers kept ordering oatmeal.

So.
Much.
Freakin'.
Oatmeal.

~~~

Table #33's phone rang. It was the same sound as my alarm. For a creepy two seconds I felt like I was being awoken from a weird waitress dream.

*****

8

Your Waitress is a Person Too

In my case, an irreverent little person with her head jammed high up in the clouds, who would rather be doing almost anything else besides showing up for a job. Often I am doing anything else but waitressing, at least mentally. Waitressing is fun most days. I enjoy the juggling of 100 different things physically, intellectually and emotionally. I need to keep busy in one of these areas or boredom nearly eats me alive. I just don't like to HAVE to waitress.

Alas, I have become accustomed to a certain type of lifestyle, one that involves not taking public transportation and being stocked up on laundry soap and toilet paper. I also like having a few days of groceries in the house and maybe buying a new pair of shoes or a pretty new dress now and again. Most importantly, my man needs an occasional hanger steak and pomme frites with béarnaise. I would be a horrible wife to deprive him of that by refusing to contribute to the family fortune.

~~~~~

My boss friend requested me on Facebook. (((((((EEEEEEKKKKKKKK)))))))))

How long do you give me before I get fired?

This is when I learned to use my privacy controls.

~~~

I wandered around the house for about 5 minutes looking for my nametag. Thank goodness I finally looked at the work shirt I was wearing, because there it was, already neatly pinned on.

~~~

All our customers except one of Dora Lee's were so nice today and we were hellaciously busy. I just got the opportunity to have a bathroom break and a peek in the mirror. It turns out my hair is a little wild and I look batshit crazy. That explains all the nice, soothing words people used with me today.

~~~

Pleasedontsitinmysectionpleasedontsitinmysectionpleasedo ntsitinmysectionpleasedontsitinmysection. Yay! The Waitress Gods heard my prayers and smiled upon me this day.

~~~

Conducting a quick mental check to make sure I am wearing every applicable item before walking into work is becoming more and more common. I don't know what to make of it.

~~~

Having to go to a J.O.B. when I would rather create sincerely harshes my buzz. You could help a girl out by purchasing a copy of her poetry book. (*The Taste of Innocence* available on Amazon. :)) If 15 of you did so, I could have a whole day off in which to loll about in pretty words that would eventually make the world a lovelier place to frolic in.

~~~

I hate to have to break out my waitress attitude this early on a Thursday.

~~~

I forgot to bring Table #54 the to-go iced tea that I so temptingly offered them. I remembered about 3 hours later.

#badwaitress

~~~

I've only been at work for 30 minutes and I have already buttered my boob and brandished a hot sausage. This is going to be a fine day.

~~~

Why does no one tell me when my hair has lept free of its restraints to flap about in an unkempt state?

~~~

Looks around hopefully for a way to get out of work today. Finding nothing, trudges out door, dejected.

~~~

Do you ever wander into work early on a Friday morning drinking a lukewarm latte out of a red solo cup, singing *Joy to the World* and then have to do a quick mental check to make sure you're wearing every necessary item of clothing? I did.

~~~

My mom came in to eat while I was working today and surprised me by singing *Happy Birthday* to me along with all the customers in my section. Very nice. :) I felt extra loved AND my tip average increased substantially. I <3 my mom.

~~~

Oops. I have arrived at work and discovered I've worn my extra high, high-water pants, short socks and I'm 2 days out from a leg shaving. Darn it.

#notimetochangenow

~~~

If only people could hear what their waitresses were thinking.

My imaginary conversation with my imaginary table:

Me: "How are you today?"

Table #5: "Good. How are you?"

Me: "Really good except that I am so hungry that my big tummy has eaten my little tummy and it is going to leap from me and eat your face soon. Also, it seems that after what one would expect to be enough years of practice, I cannot get my bra hooked on the 3rd hook this week and my girls feel hyper insecure. I am insanely uncomfortable and my coworker Rose may be sick of me trying to jiggle them into place. I will fix them in the break room soon. Also, I have to pee. Can I get you some coffee?"

~~~

I am hot sticky sweet. Not in the good way.

~~~

I often have lengthy conversations with people with whom I have no idea what the fuck they're saying. They never notice.

#ENUNCIATEplease #justoneofmymanyskillz

~~~

It is hellaciously stupid that I am wasting my time being a waitress, as fun as it might be.

~~~

There is a very good chance that your waitress has to pee.

~~~

I will physically attend work. Mentally, I will be dancing barefoot through a sun-warmed meadow whilst appreciatively smelling a handful of white daisies. That is all.

~~~

Note to self: A work apron is the last item of clothing to put on, not the second. Focus woman!

~~~

This morning is one of those mornings where I am hyper aware of the fact that having to go to a job day after day in order to make money so that my family and I may survive is a very stupid system. I protest this workday.

~~~

Heading into work and hoping that I don't have donut residue on my pudgy little face.

~~~

Table #61: "Does your husband call you Angel? My Angel?"

Me: "No. I've killed all the romance."

~~~

I have executed my first eye roll of the day. I have only been working 9 minutes.

~~~

I feel extra warm and fuzzy when the girls at work are whispering feverishly and they do not stop when I get close.

~~~

I am stuck at work with one of those slidey bra straps. I am seriously thinking about pulling it out my sleeve and going about my day like nothing is amiss.

~~~

The damn elastic must've snapped on my underwear because they have been falling down all day and I've been stuck at work unable to fix the problem. I have the song *London Bridge is Falling Down* stuck in my head, only I am singing slightly different words. Yeah.

~~~

I have, for 2 hours, had one of those boogers stuck in my nose that tickles whenever I breathe in or out. I am at work. No lady-like method has worked to extract it. I am not amused.

Ok, I am a little amused.

~~~

I think I may go on a bender instead of schleppin' out pie today.

~~~

I wonder if Table #61 heard my stomach growling.

~~~

Focus Angel. PantsfirstthenapronPANTSfirstTHENapron. Geez.

~~~

My work pants are too high and my socks are too short. Every time I feel the breeze on my ankles, it makes me giggle.

~~~

I'm watching my handsome husband sort and count the mad stacks of cash I brought home this week. It's been going on for like 10 minutes. Damn! I waitressed my ass off. The song *I'm a Woman* is playing in my mind. (If you Google it, it's the Enjoli version.)

~~~

I've made an uncomfortable amount of eye contact with the man at Table #12.

#yourwaitressissincere

~~~

Looking in my visor mirror on the way to work, I discovered tiny tomato sauce stains on each side of my mouth left over from the lasagna I had for breakfast. How am I an adult?

~~~

I work at 8:15. I decided to get ready at 8. You can probably see where my math went wrong, yet I arrived with 3 minutes to spare. It seems I've made time my bitch this day. Woot!

~~~

I'm mid talking to Table #53 and I burp while I'm talking. A dainty, ladylike burp, but still...

~~~

Me: "Would you like pie today?"

Table #30: "You're going to hell for tempting."

Me: "I'm going to hell for a lot worse than that."

~ ~ ~

I am such a stellar employee that I showed up an hour early to work. F$!# ! Back home.

Sigh.

~ ~ ~

I worked for 2 hours before I realized I had 2 aprons on. Now I'm wearing them for fun.

~ ~ ~

I am sweaty and sticky. I'm wearing whipped cream, some unidentifiable sauce-like stuff and I smell of disillusionment and unfulfilled dreams. I learned things today that I can never unlearn. Ever. I feel my work is done. The good news is my headache is gone. I am clocking out. No more waitressing today.

*****

Angel Woolery

9

The Flirty, the Dirty,
and the Perty

Three cheers for the uninhibited!! I love the freaks! I truly do. Fly your freak flag high and proud! That said, I must tell you in all honesty that your waitress does not want to date you. Probably. Usually. I did marry the hot guy from Table #62, so sometimes it could happen I guess. It doesn't hurt to try once or twice, but after that, let it rest. She also doesn't want to see your man junk. She won't call that number you left. A big tip will not change her mind. Flirting is fine unless you're gross. Ass grabbing is not ok. In fact, don't touch your waitress anywhere without permission. I cannot even count the number of uninvited gropings, hugs, ass slappings, kisses, attempted fondlings and good lord, you name its, I have been on the receiving end of.

Because I am good natured, I usually smile and walk away quickly, but if you do this to the wrong waitress, you will regret it.

~~~~~

Table #24 insists that I called him a Studmuffin once. I totally don't remember it, but he is very pleased about it all.

~~~

I got a winker at Table# 24. I love getting winked at!

~~~

The dude at Table #60 looked like he was gonna go ahead and have me for lunch.

~~~

I assumed that the universe knew that the only frisky old man penis I would ever wish to see would be my husband's in another 40 years or so. But no. The whole, entire tip and a good inch or two more of Table #64's 70+ year old mucho grande wang-a-lang was peeking out from the daisy dukes he was sporting.

MY EYES! BLEACH!! I NEED BLEACH!!

After 3 pieces of pie, numerous requests running me for things, and no attempt to stuff that sucker back in his drawers, he hollered over to me, "You're a sweetie! Come over here, I got a tip for you!" At which point a loud squeak escaped me. The first squeak of my entire life.

I have never squashed down so many mad giggles in my whole life. Many thanks to my co-worker Dora Lee for her unwavering emotional support while this played out, even though she wouldn't go look.

Henceforth, he shall be known as Penis Man.

~~~

Table #60 had semi-discreet parking lot sex on the trunk of their car before coming in to quench their other appetites. (Yes, we watched.)

They didn't even wash their hands when they were done. Gross.

They came a few times. To the restaurant I mean, not on the trunk of the car.

~~~

Table #34 has a teardrop tattooed under his eye. I've never seen that in real life. It's fascinating. I cannot stop staring.

~~~

I was waiting on a hot deaf guy at Table #64 and it comes time to ask if he would like pie. Stumped, I could think of no appropriate sign for pie. I should have done the one I thought of because it made me happy, and it probably would've made him happy too.

~~~

I feel awkward every time the grown woman at Table #53 uses her cutesy voice on me. Is this how men feel?

~~~

Young man at Table #60 says to me, "I'm a sucker for a warm muffin."

I stood there and stared like a deer in headlights as I struggled to filter through the many options I could reply with. I opted for a safe reply. Lame, but safe.

The mental challenge has left me weary.

~~~

I flipped off our cook, Esteban. I don't think it effectively translates into Spanish. He keeps wiggling his eyebrows at me.

~~~

I'm a die-hard fan of leather chaps, but the guy at Table #62 should have consulted someone before getting into his.

~~~

The old dude at Table #62 kept trying to tickle me while I passed with full trays.

~~~

Table #61 left a phone number. I wasn't even flirting. My sexy must be powerful strong today.

~~~

I was talking with a customer about SCUBA diving. I told her I was most worried about sharks. She said that what I needed to NOT do is put my hand in any hole, because an eel could bite me, and that really I should not put anything in any hole that I wouldn't want to lose.

I told her that was good advice for any day.

#unintentionalnaughtiness #Oops.

~~~

Me: "Would you like me to warm your muffin?"

Ninety year old woman: "A warm muffin is always good."
There was a distinct twinkle in her eye when she said it.

~~~

Table #83 politely asked me for a hug, so I obliged. His
friend expressed dismay that he did not also get a hug. So I
traded tray hands and gave him a big hug and a lapful of icy
water.

It turns out I cannot stand on one foot, bent over,
hugging, while using my non-tray hand to balance glasses.
Who knew?

~~~

I feel my coworkers deeply misunderstood my desire to
work at a toy store.

~~~

One of my regulars keeps asking me to go out for coffee
with him and I keep telling him no. One day he tipped me
$80 and he only had a beverage. I thanked him. I am polite
after all.

Customer: "Will you have coffee with me today?"

Me: "No. Do you want your tip back?"

Customer: "No, that's ok."

Creepy, but I kept the money. It's rude to turn down a tip.

~~~

Table #35 has so much ear hair that all I can think of when I walk by is, 'Only you can prevent forest fires.'

~~~

Table #51 to me: "Hello pretty."

Sweet talk like that will get you the awesomest piece of pie.

~~~

The hot guy at Table #61 is making solid eye contact with me. It's making me giddy. I'll probably end up spilling something on him.

~~~

This 75-85ish year old regular decided it would be a good idea to write me a lengthy, dirty note while his wife was out of town. It included, but was not limited to, talking about what type of fabric I prefer the panties I wear to be fashioned from and when my birthday was. I'm guessing so that he could get me a sexy present at the appropriate time, or so he could have some special happy time by himself later while thinking about it. The latter gives me uncontrollable jeebies.

I did not give him the note back when he requested it and instead shared it with my manager and coworkers so I didn't have to be horrified all by myself, and also so they knew who to start questioning should I come up missing. Sick bastard. I applaud the generous size of the cojones it must have taken for him to carry out his plan, but in the doing of it, he went from one of my very favorite regulars to someone I now avoid with all my might.

~~~

I'm hard pressed not to motor-boat Table #53's generous and prominently displayed assets.

~~~

I got a winker at Table #13. Yay!

Me: "Are you doing good?"

Winker at Table #13: (making direct eye contact) "I'm doing great Angel. Thanks."

#waitressmagicinprogress

~~~

Table #24 dude was looking at my boobs. Each. Individually.

~~~

Table #63 invited me to a night of gambling and a threesome. She was serious.

Tempting…Not.

I declined. Politely, because I have good manners and it's not like they were insulting me.

Yikes.

~~~

The old guy at Table #34 is sporting an Andy Gibb style haircut. It's making me all tingly.

~~~

I must have greeted Table #11 a little too intensely because now he's making the sexy eyes.

I escaped before he worked up enough courage. Muahahaha!!!

~~~

I am usually immune to the sexy of strangers, but Table #51, a long-haired, rocker dude well into his 50s, started flinging his sexy around. He was talking in his deep, raspy voice, focusing completely on me. While trying to not titter like a schoolgirl, I walked into a wall.
Thankfully, he did not see.

~~~

Some old dude gave me a double-cheeked whack on the butt with his cane today. Rock on old dude!

I let him get by with this because truly, I love him and his friend. They come in regularly and shoot the shit with each other and the staff when we've time. They are always mannerly.

They tip respectably and they bring others in every once in a while. They're a little rowdy and fun and one of them calls me Sweet Pea. I adore them. Whack away frisky critters, I'll whoop like a barmaid from yesteryear every time.

~~~

I may have smiled too sincerely at the man at Table #50 because now instead of happy and flirty, he looks hopeful and a tad lecherous.

~~~

I was sorely tempted to run my fingers through Table #60's delightful chest carpet but fear of a hefty gold chain and/or medallion injury kept me from it.

~~~

I must've put the emphasis on the wrong syllable as I gestured toward the picture of pie and said, "You want that bad boy?"

Table #68 man looks surprised and says, "What?!"

I giggled as I realized what I had done.

He may be in more often now.

~~~

I did not know I had a sexy walk. Thank you random customer man. :)

~~~

I'm confounded that men feel free to touch my butt. WHY?? WHY?? Is there a sign on it?

~~~

I am getting winked at by the old guy at Table #43. What a cutie pie.

~~~

I got busted checkin' out the hottie at Table #12. Are shorts that short even legal on a grown man?

~~~

I thought I was handling, quite professionally, a hot, long-haired guy's charms. Indeed, I made it right up to offering pie before I started giggling like a school girl. He left $5. :)

~~~

A dirty old man at Table #63 told me: "You can take my check if you reach into my pocket and get my wallet out."

Wow. Tempting.

*****

10

Allergies and Special Diets

Please don't lie about an allergy. We can tell and we talk about you in the back of the house. As wait staff, we take your health very seriously. If you have an allergy, we will do our best to accommodate it. If you have an allergy to a food that will kill you if you eat it, we will even go into the freezer during the dinner rush to read the ingredient label. A dead customer is not a return customer after all. It would be nice if you called ahead or looked online though, because label reading in the freezer when we are busy is a pain in the ass and it will not earn you any kind thoughts.

~~~~~

The question: "Would you like corn bread, focaccia bread or a dinner roll?"

Says Table #63 woman adamantly and a little bitchily, "I do not eat bread!" As she scarfs down her crouton laden salad and wheat covered fries with breaded chicken strips on the way.

Whatever lady! *Makes large mental W with hands in mind*

~~~

No! I will not take the 5 almond slivers off the top of your banana cream pie. Lazy ass.

Get to picking.

~~~

It seems that Table #66 is allergic to bread. Not wheat. Bread.

~~~

Table #11 explained at length how she could not have eggs because she was allergic to dairy. Then she snarfed down a slice of banana cream pie.

Rudimentary knowledge of food groups is beneficial if one wishes to not appear a complete idiot while discussing dietary needs. Just sayin'.

~~~

Table #53 man: "I can't have broccoli, I'd like celery instead."

Me: (After much discussion in the kitchen) "You can have it today but may not be able to every time."

Table #53 wife: "He can't have green vegetables."

Me: "Celery is green."

Table #53 man: "No it's not."

Me: "It's not?"

Table #53 wife: "No. It's not."

Me: "Huh."

~~~

Table #52 is allergic to coleslaw.

~~~

Table #64 requested sugar free syrup from me because she is diabetic. She put it on her cinnamon roll french toast and pancake. I'm confused.

~~~

Table #50 says he's allergic to mayonnaise.

~~~

A messy haired man in sherbet orange pants boldly announced he has issues with nuts!

He did not specify what kind of nuts. I asked no questions.

~~~

Table #51 is allergic to bacon.

I think a telethon is in order to help find a cure. Of all the things to be unable to eat, this is by far the worst! Tragic.

~~~

The poor little boy at Table #60 is allergic to corn syrup. That must be a tough one!

~~~

Table #64 woman: "Can they leave out the green peppers? They don't like me."

Me: "Sure."

Then, when delivering the food...

Me: "No green peppers so you can have a good day today!"

Table #64 guy: "It's not the day I'm worried about. It's tonight."

~~~

Table #63: "I want scrambled eggs, hash browns and white toast."

I repeat the order back.

Table #63: "Please tell the cook I am allergic to onions. I had my waitress tell him last time and it worked. My eggs were perfect."

WAITRESS

Me: *seriously reexamining my choice of profession*

*****

Angel Woolery

11

Cheap Fuckers

If you're going to stiff me, at least have the decency to tell me I'm pretty first.

~~~~~

My eye got a little twitchy when Table #62 sent me to break a dollar into 4 quarters in order to tip me.

~~~

Table #10

Yes, you can split the pie. That is acceptable. No, you may not split your coffee!

~~~

I just recognized Table #23. Last time they tipped me in crafts. I swear to God I will smack them if I get ANYTHING made out of Popsicle sticks. FML! I am in waitress hell right now.

After wasting my time with banal chatter throughout their entire 3 hour stay, and me only escaping because sometimes I was willing to walk away mid-sentence, they called me back for some syrupy verbal tipping. The woman tells me they don't have enough money for a tip, but she made some Halloween cards and would like me to have one. It was pretty and it took a lot of time so I graciously accepted both the card and the fact that I really didn't need what would have likely been a dollar from them anyway.

That is, until I returned to the dining room to find that she had given out a stack of her handmade cards to a table of teenagers. Then, I didn't feel so fucking special.

Verbal tip- Using words in lieu of a cash tip. The words contain effusive praise for the wonderful service and all around stellar dining experience, for the quality of the food, the glorious red of the ketchup, or the way the bubbles in the soda have never been as wonderfully bubbly ever, anywhere. It's ridiculous, it's annoying and it's a waste of time.

Words do not pay the bills. Servers recognize this a mile away and it makes them want to do violence.

~~~

I wonder if Table #50 is trying to tempt me to excellence by leaving that dollar out where I can see it.

~~~

There is a large group of people that have been coming in regularly for years. They all pay separately, they all tip separately. I wait on them and when they leave, I clear the table and collect the tips. That is the polite way to do it.

The last few times they have been in however, many of them tell me to "pick up my tips," "here honey, why don't you collect that money up," "make sure you get your tips." Heck! A few of them have been putting the cash right into my hand. Odd behaviour. Curiosity got the better of me.

I finally had to whisper one of them: "Is someone stealing the tips?"

Customer: "Mmmhmmm."

Me: "Do you know who it is?"

Customer: "Mmmhmmm."

I look towards the person a few seats away and whisper, "Is it her?"

Customer: "Mmmhmmm."

Me: "Good to know. Thanks!"

She also steals the jelly packets.

~~~

Table #63 got perfect service and left $2 on a $55 tab. I am not thinking kind thoughts.

~~~

My thoughts on tips:

If you can afford to go out to eat, you can afford to tip. If you can't, eat at home. You make your waitress sad.

The only time you should tip nothing is if you are horribly unhappy with your dining experience, it was your server's fault and nothing was done to make it right. It happens. If it happens to you a lot, examine your behaviour because the odds are high that it is you messing things up.

Tip on the pre-discount price. This means tip on the full amount of your check BEFORE anything is taken off. That is what servers have to claim on their taxes. The government doesn't care if you have a coupon or get a free meal. They want their money and so do we. The work required is still the same.

Do not tip less than you pay in tax. It really hurts our feelings.

If you request special changes to your food, a birthday song, have messy children, are needy or cause extra work for the wait or kitchen staff, tip extra.

A tip for regular service - 15%

A tip for good service - 20%

WAITRESS

A tip for the waitress that makes your day wonderful and delivers unto you the best service of your life, tip what your heart tells you to (but not less than 20%!).

*****

Angel Woolery

12

More Nice Customers

Again, yes. Because these people are the majority and they deserve to be recognized.

I cannot possibly give proper written loving acknowledgment to the thousands of excellent examples of humanity I have had the pleasure of meeting and waiting on over the course of my career, but they know who they are. I always take extra time and care for the nice customers and when I am very lucky, I make a new friend that stays with me throughout this journey called my life.

~~~~~

In my early years of waitressing I had a lovely customer named Clem. He used to tip me and then he would leave extra "Bambino" money. A $2 bill, a Kennedy 1/2 dollar, things like this for the baby. I was not pregnant for a good many years yet at that point, but I saved it all in a cute little pencil box and I have added to it. That box is stuffed full! It turns out that my boy is a saver and a planner. Clem must have known. While he passed away long before my sweet baby was even a twinkle in my eye, Clem is still a dear part of my life, living in my heart as a sweet memory. <3

~~~

Me: "I'm Angel. I'll be your server."

Table #62: "I've had you before. You're good!"

~~~

All my customers were super nice today. The highlight for me was when I overheard a lady tell her friend I was slim.

Slim may be a stretch, but it was nice to hear.

~~~

I hear Table #62 as I'm walking away, "That's Angel. She's one of the nice ones."

Ha!! Damn straight.

~~~

Me (Showing a picture to regulars): "This is my boy. He's 12."

Table #67 gasped, "What?! Were you, like, 10 when you had him??"

Me: *blush*

~~~

A stranger picked up the tab for one of my party tables AND he left me a $27 tip.

I love it when someone is kind enough to pick up the tab of a stranger. It happens every few months or so and it's wonderful to see the surprise on the faces of the benefitting customers!

I highly recommend doing this at least once or twice a year. It will make you and many others feel great!

~~~

Table #34 said I am AMAZING.

~~~

Table #66: "You are one of the best waitresses we've ever had."

~~~

Table #65 to Me: "YOU ARE AWESOME!"

Thank ya kindly Table #65. You are too.

~~~

Table #51 woman: (Reaches to hug me, thinks better of it and takes my hand instead.)

Me: "You can hug me. I like you."

Table #51 woman: "I like you too." (She gave me a big hug.)

~~~

The sweet old lady at Table #54 said I was a cute little thing.

~~~

Table #66 to me: "You are very good at what you do."

Thank you Table #66, I love you too!

~~~

One of my regulars told me I was inspirational. I don't know why, but it was very sweet of her to say.

~~~

The lovely ladies at Table #65 kept telling me how pretty my name was and how nice it was that my mom could always call me "her Angel". Then, while I was cleaning another table, I heard one call out, "Angel!" I go over and one of them is giggling and she says to the other, "See, she even looks like an Angel." I love nice customers!!

~~~

When I walked up to Table #33, she says to her friend, "Yay! We get Angel!"

~~~

Table #60 woman to me: "My husband says you have a delightful personality and I just wanted to pass that along to you."

~~~

Table #64 came in with my name already written on their coupon. They had wanted to remember what waitress to ask for.

sparkles

~~~

Table #55 got there about 10 minutes before me this morning. They flagged me down when they were done eating and asked, "What time do you usually get here in the morning?"

Me: "8ish."

Table #55: "Dang! We just missed you. We like your service best. We'll come in later next week."

~~~

My favorite story from work today:

I'm ringing in an order and from behind me I heard a customer yoohoo into the server aisle, "Waitress..."

I brace myself and turn to find the smiling face of one of my awesome regulars and I breathe a sigh of relief. She waves a $20 at me and says, "This is for you in case I don't see you again. I want you to know how much we appreciate you. I'm going to Florida for the winter. I'll be back in May."

I gave her a big hug and a thank you. That was super nice and unexpected.

*****

13

Holidays

If I am not working, I love holidays. If I am, fuck holidays.

If you must go out to eat on a holiday, remember that a nice fat tip takes away a little of the pain your waitress feels having to work instead of being home with her family.

~~~~~

*Thanksgiving

We are not a 24 hour store. Except this one day. This one time.

I head into work at midnight on turkey day because greedy corporate jerks feel like running specials ON a holiday and must need the few extra hundred they're going to make because of it. Seriously. Are people still hungry? I do not believe rousting a middle-aged woman from her turkey coma is justified. I was up at 7am preparing a feast and it will be a 24 hour day by the time I'm done. I suspect I will be bored as fuck tonight. Expect some complaining.

2:23 am. 2 1/2 hours in. No table yet. Drank an iced tea. Drank a medium latte. Peed twice. Ate pie. Earned the hell out of my $7.25 an hour. The place damn near sparkles.

3:06 am. 3 hours in and still, no table. I ate a piece of bacon. I did not pay for it. It is my "bonus bacon" for hauling my ass out on a cold, unforgiving evening to work for minimum wage. I may have another in 30 minutes.

3:35 am. 3 1/2 hours in. Peed again. Had another piece of bacon. Sustained a horrible pie box paper cut on my pinkie finger that damn near made me bleed out and I just got my first table.

2 1/2 stupid hours to go.

4:08 am. 4 stupid hours into a useless shift. Had apple cider. Peeing. My life is so exciting. Gotta stop with all the liquid. Awake for 21 hours with a little nap. Getting delirious.

4:35 am. FML. 4 1/2 hours in. I have spent more than I've made. I have to pee again.

Not gonna do it. Holding it now for entertainment and so I don't fall asleep. Ate cucumber slices topped with ranch and croutons. Had more cider.

5:03 am. 5 hours into this shift. I just got my second table. Starting to do the potty dance.

Found out someone will not be in for their morning shift and that I might have to stay late. I will no doubt be driven to violence. I will not be staying late if it is not busy.

5:39 am. 5 1/2 hours in. Ate cranberry nut oatmeal. Gave up trying not to pee. Hopefully it's almost over.

5:53 am. Scheduled 'til 6. Had enough at 5:50. Me and my 3 dollars let my boss know that I was done and I was leaving. Going home to sleep so sweetly.

~~~

I got my first Christmas tip of the season! Yay!! I LOVE ME SOME holiday tips.

~~~

Some of my honey pie regulars left me such a generous Xmas tip, that it made me feel a little bashful.

~~~

I am going to wear my boingy Santa hat to work. It's dazzling.

It is a normal Santa hat with a foot tall wobbling, bouncing, swaying, jingle bell bedecked velvety coil jutting straight out the top. It makes me happy.

~~~

I wonder why the lady at Table #12 suggested a way to silence my pretty jingle bells?

Table #12 lady is affectionately called Nurse Ratched around these parts. I did not gift her with the name but it suits her. She occasionally brings in her young grandchildren. I feel so bad for them. She nags them continuously and at high volume about embarrassing things throughout their stay. There is no happiness left inside of her except possibly when she has sucked the remaining joy out of all within the range of her voice. Then, her eyes twinkle briefly, like a mosquito hitting a bug zapper.

~~~

My faith in humanity has been restored by a stellar Christmas tip! I LOVE Christmas tips!

~~~

*Christmas Day

Just a heads up:

1. I have to work today.

2. I do not want to.

3. I'm a little cranky about it but I'm on a holiday high, which may or may not temper my hourly bitching about it.

4. I imagine it will be as slow as Santa Claus in a post-Christmas cookie stupor.

~~~

Table #22: "I'm sorry you have to work on Christmas."

Me: "Thank you. It's ok."

Table #22: "Thanks for being cheerful about it!"

Me: "I'm drunk."

~~~

I gave up bitching for Lent. I made it all the way to 1:15.

My sister in-law likes to remind me I'm not Catholic. Once a year, I give it a try.

~~~

*Mother's Day

I kindly volunteered to work yesterday, Mother's Day. I hate working on Mother's Day.

This year, I figured I would let one of my coworkers with a younger child bask in the glow of love focused completely on her for a day.

Never again.

For starters, it is insanely busy. All the women who come in get a free dessert, which adds to the workload. They also get a free carnation, which I think is totally lame AND adds to the work load. While it is a nice gesture, it's a cheap carnation, nothing more. Children should be giving the flowers, not the waitress. We also run out before 3:00pm every year and some women are very upset by this. Seriously. I don't want to hear it. I am not the boss of flower purchasing. We are only allotted so many by our corporate overlords.

After hours of unrelenting wild children and adoring husbands, there was finally light at the end of the server aisle and I had a moment to breathe. That is when my own mom, my mother in law, my son and my husband come in for a bite and to throw a little needed love my way. I got them drinks and took their order and then I have to ignore them for a while because I was still busy, but not crazy busy. They are my most patient customers because they love me, because they hear me bitch colorfully after a rotten shift and they know I am sometimes close to the edge of sanity. I may have looked near to said edge upon their arrival.

While trying to say a few words to them, the adjacent table waved me over. One of the guests did not get the correct sandwich. I took it back to the kitchen for what should have been a quick fix. After about 10 minutes, I ask the cook where it is. He points to a new order and what is most definitely not the correct sandwich. Again. Frustrated, but maintaining my composure, he begins to remake it. Again. I apologize to the guest profusely. Again. Everyone at his table is almost done eating.

Another 10 minutes pass and I am sure I've ruined the guest's day. I cannot talk to my own family because then it looks like I am ignoring the table with the order trouble. I am emotionally drained from the previous 5 hours of hell and I go back for likely the tenth time and ask if the sandwich is almost done. The cook (who is usually one of my favorites) says that yes, he is finishing it. He puts it up in the window, and it is the wrong damn sandwich.

I burst into immediate, loud, uncontrollable, overwrought waitress tears. The cook looks horrified but amused as he puts the correct one up and tells me he was only joking. Too late. I've lost my damn mind. My hiccupping sobs, loud sniffling and red face may be the only thing that saved me from a serious tongue lashing at the table as I brought out the correct sandwich long after everyone else had finished eating.

We took the meal off the check of course.

Every year I forget how horrible it is to work on Mother's Day and I agree to work it.

Never again. I was cured. Screw Mother's Day.

*****

Angel Woolery

14

Biosafety Level Two:
Gases, Fluids, and Solids

I take my life into my hands when going out amongst my tables. Biohazards abound and I feel defenseless in my ungloved, unmasked state. After all these years of being at the mercy of germy strangers, my immune system is remarkable but not unfellable. Do your waitress and fellow humans a favor and dispose of your needles and other medical waste in the proper fashion. I don't want to pick up your bloody bandages or pus streaked gauze. If you are sick, for God's sake, don't go out to eat. Have you ever watched a slow motion video of the snot spray that sneezing produces? Or the spew of fluids from coughing? It's vile.

There is more poop, puke and urine than you'd ever really want to know about in the restaurant business. I get it, things happen. Bodies produce moist, gross, smelly substances. Sometimes by surprise. Just don't leave it for your waitress. That's all I'm asking.

~~~~~

In the dish pit after pre-bussing, I found a small syringe needle swimming in the leftover ranch dressing of a 2 oz. ramekin, compliments of Table #53. I returned it to him with a sweet smile and a raised eyebrow, and told him we did not have proper disposal facilities and he'd have to take it with him.

He and his wife expressed surprise that it could not be left hidden in the pile of dirty dishes, thrown away by the waitress to later stab the person who takes out the trash.

I hope HE gets stabbed by the tainted needle of a stranger. Then maybe he will "remember" biohazard protocol for all eternity.

~~~

Three cheers for a napkin dotted liberally with dabbed off zit blood.

~~~

The dude at Table #62 stuck his whole damn arm almost up to his elbow, into his pants, to better scratch his man berries. He's like 25 years old. As a bonus, he made a groaning noise as he did so.

His grandma, (yes, his grandma was with him) shook her head gently and smiled as if to say, "Boys will be boys."

Were that my grandson, I would have thunked him in the head with the backside of my spoon, apologized profusely for his behaviour and sent him to wash his hands. Then I would have hustled him out of there dragging the shameful stench of mortification along behind me like a smallpox infested blanket, never to return again.

Henceforth, he shall be known as 'Ballscratcher'.

~~~

Nothing expresses to your waitress how much you love her quite as thoroughly as a wadded up, blood spotted napkin nestled atop the pretty tortilla strips on your used appetizer plate.

~~~

The woman being sat at Table #68 noticed something dark on the back fabric of the booth. She did the only reasonable thing she could do and ran her hand through it, brought it to her nose for identification purposes and then recoiled in horror. Poop.

~~~

Thanks Table #51 for leaving the crumpled up, booger-filled tissue.

~~~

Today I may have done the single most disturbing thing I have ever done in the entirety of my waitress career. I probably won't die. Probably.

Two sweet old lady regulars told me that their hash browns were very salty. One gave me her whole plate to take away. The other told me she really wanted me to taste them, plucked a wad of them off her plate (from the untouched side) and handed them to me. Something that was on her plate. That she touched with her bare fingers. So I tasted, because I am a good waitress and because seemingly, I have no fear for my personal safety. I promptly spit the salty taters out.

They were right. Now I know.

~~~

Table #34 left me a surgical tape wrapped chunk of gauze.

~~~

Every time she comes in, Table #35 pees her pants while sitting on the fabric-bottomed booth. We sanitize it after every visit but the pee smell is starting to stick to the clothing of others when they sit there. It is permanent now. Only new upholstery will handle the stench.

I feel bad for this gal as the Alzheimer's is setting in hard, but it's too much. She has to stop coming in.

~~~

Table #43 left a used bag of "Mother's Milk". I'm all for breastfeeding, but boob food is a body fluid and waitresses are not keen to pick up any juiciness that came out of any hole you own. Just sayin'.

~~~

I want to know - at what point did it become socially acceptable to say, "I need to be seated close to the bathroom"? Ick ick ick!!! Stay home people!!

This could just be a personal irritation and I may be too judgy, it's true, but this is what I am thinking:

1. They're going to be eating something that disagrees with them so badly that they know they will need to make a run for it. No food is worth explosive diarrhea. Ever.

2. They have had hot, ass burning nastiness blowing out of them all day and while being held hostage by the porcelain butt cradle, began to fantasize about pumping greasy meat and sugary desserts into their bodies as if that could not possibly be what's causing the anal vomiting to begin with. They are sitting close to the bathroom so their dreams can be realized without spraying their fellow diners with steamy regret. Polite. But still, no.

3. Bathroom fetish.

All disgusting.

Which reminds me of a man and woman that used to come in to the restaurant: I was, only once, witness to what I am about to tell you, but I am assured that it has happened on several different occasions.

I was waiting on a nice couple in their mid-60s to early 70s. They seemed normal enough. They politely ate their food, paid the bill and went to use the facilities before continuing on their merry way. I would never have spared them a further thought had they not broken out their batshit crazy in the middle of the dinner rush.

Somewhere between using the facilities and going on their merry way, they both, in each bathroom, simultaneously smeared feces all over the toilet, walls and floor. And not just the bathroom floor. They tracked their shit onto the dining room carpet for about 10 feet until the contents on their shoes had been exhausted. Then, the vile pair walked out as if nothing were amiss. Why they have not been banned from dining with us is a complete mystery to me.

Side note: Never let your children play on the carpeted floor of a public place. I've seen some things, man. Crazy, nasty, vile things.

~~~

Table #52 left a well-used, brownish yellow wax coated cotton swab.

~~~

I win for grossest thing found at work today! A long, glittery, press on nail that had seen better days. I was parading it around triumphantly when Dora Lee says, "Imagine all the old lady cooter goo encrusted on that!" Dora Lee wins for grossest thing said all day! I washed my hands thoroughly.

~~~

As Penis Man's friend handed me my hard-earned tip, I fleetingly wondered how much old man ball sweat I inadvertently touch in a day because of poor hand washing habits on the part of my old man customers.

#cantstopit   #mymentalhamsterruns24/7

~~~

The woman at Table #35 is picking at the many scabs on her face.

shudder

~~~

Table #74 is lounging in his own fart cloud, giving me his order and pretending nothing is amiss.

~~~

The woman sitting at Table #64 is wearing a skirt and sitting with her knees spread 2 feet apart like a good ole boy.

No one wants to see your cooter, lady.

~~~

Me: "Would you like an iced tea or perhaps coffee to start with?"

Table #63 lady: "Nothing now. Please come back. I have a sick eye."

~~~

I'm so happy today. Even the woman clipping her nails at Table #33 can't kill my buzz!

*Nail clipping in a restaurant. It's gross. Why? A piece could fly wildly through the air as nail clippings are wont to do, and land in someone's food or drink. Also, because it's gross.
Please groom yourself at home.*

~~~

Table #43 left a wadded up, dirty diaper on top of their plate.

~~~

Table #32 lady is wearing so much baby powder that not only can I smell it, I think that if I start smacking her, ginormous puffs will rise off of her and fill the dining room in an unnavigable fog.

~~~

I started to tell my husband about something gross a customer did at work.

Me: "What's the dirtiest thing in a restaurant?"

My husband: "The waitress?"

Me: (Ok, he got me on that one.) "The second dirtiest?"

The gross thing: Two young mothers were in with 2 babies, both around a year or so old. When I approached the table to get their drink order, I see an open menu in front of one of the babies. Dumped out on it, is a juicy, chunky fruit cup. The baby is eating off it. The horror must have shown clearly upon my face because the mom, who misread the meaning of that look on my face said, "Oh! Don't worry! I'll clean it off."

That baby may end up with the plague.

~~~

The man at Table #31 let rip two of the loudest farts I have ever heard. Part of the noise may have been the vibration of the noxious cloud as it forcefully escaped his butthole and threatened the booth fabric. I will check for fabric tears when the toxins have cleared.

~~~

The dude at Table #63 has dried blood all over his thumb and index finger and no visible wound. I don't even want to know.

~~~

My manager had to low crawl, G.I. Joe style, under a bathroom stall door because some old chick couldn't figure out how to work the simple partition slide bolt latch that is industry standard.

~~~

My first table of the day stuck her finger in her ear and dug quite efficiently. She must have gotten something real good because when she extracted her finger, she had to clean under her fingernail.

~~~

Table #62 was sitting sideways in the booth with his back against the wall and his legs stretched out along the seat, drunk. We were in the middle of a rush. As I was flying by, I turned my head to look to make sure that he was doing all right. In that exact moment, drunk dude projectile vomited all the way to his feet.

It felt like slow motion as I watched in horror while the contents of his stomach emptied. I didn't miss a step however. There was no time. I went into the back, grabbed a towel, went back out to the dining room, tossed it at him and said, "Clean it up."

~~~

Table #71 is knuckle deep in his left nostril. Yum.

~~~

Table #68 injected her insulin while I was standing there. Her bloody sterile wipe thingy is sitting on the table grossing me out while she sheaths her needle. Just so we are clear: A person's body fluids are only not gross to the person themselves, maybe close friends and family and to medical professionals wearing proper gear. To me, any bloody, snotty, moist or fluid covered things look like herp infested, phlegm covered, squirrel nesting that I wouldn't want to touch with a blowtorch being held by a friend. Please pass along this information concerning good manners to your secreting, sneezing, bleeding, coughing, leaky, flesh poking, juicy friends.

On behalf of waitresses everywhere, thank you.

~~~

Ooo yummy! A blood soaked square of gauze was awaiting me as I cleared Table #41.

~~~

The guy at Table #31 has a big slimy loogie imbedded in his mustache. It's making me gag to look at it.

~~~

I do not even want to know why booth #55 smelled so strongly of Braunschweiger long after the occupants had left. We do not serve it.

~~~

Do I tell the woman about the poop stain on the ass seam of her light tan pants?

No. No, I do not. She either didn't wipe well, sat in an unfortunate puddle of questionable stuff that happened to end up strategically placed, or she sharted. I cannot come to terms with it nor do I want to. Poop stain woman is on her own today.

~~~

I could say much about Table #66 but I think the fact that they left food covered floss behind says enough!

~~~

I don't understand what compels a grown man to jam his thumb up his nose to dig for a booger while he is in public. Thanks Table #51 man. Thanks a lot.

~~~

I waited on the juiciest, most secretious people I have ever had the misfortune to serve today. If I mentally revisit this day even one more time, I may hurl.

~~~

The ill-tempered, icky woman at Table #54 brought a book to the bathroom with her.

~~~

Table #64 has a little extra time to kill this morning so she has gotten out her magnifying mirror and has been picking contentedly at her face for the last 10 minutes.

~~~

Thanks Table #33 for leaving the wound dressing behind.

~~~

I really, really, really wish my customers would STOP leaving behind things that have body fluids on them. Please.

~~~

Table #34 has what is most likely a tiny, little booger attached to the end of an inch long hair, hanging out of his nostril. You're welcome.

~~~

No one wants to hear about your "drainage problem" Table #35. In the future, please use the texting option on your cell phone.

~~~

I think that if I can smell someone's ass long after they leave their booth, they should maybe try to wipe a little deeper.

~~~

Table #43 left not one, not two, not three, but four floss sticks on the table. Yum.

#groupflossing #retireddentists?

~~~

I had the distinct pleasure of walking through someone's omelette fueled fart cloud. I really should know better as he tells us regularly about his bowel issues, but I was distracted.

~~~

I was lucky enough to wait on someone that requested a table next to the bathroom! Yay for me! AND they were kind enough to leave a blood smeared napkin on top of their dirty plates for me to dispose of. WTF?! REALLY? Do I need to wear gloves and carry disinfectant to serve chicken strips?

~~~

How does one miss the whole toilet and actually shit a pile onto the floor? How? Then someone, perhaps the shitter herself, didn't see it and stepped in it, leaving a neat little trail of shitty footprints. How can someone not see a big pile of shit?

~~~

It has been nearly 12 hours and I am still troubled by having had to pick the surgical tape laden cotton ball off the syrup drenched plate. Thank you Table #54. Tonight's horrifying, sweat ridden, angst inducing 3am waitress nightmare is dedicated to you.

~~~~~

Angel Woolery

15

Little Fuckers

Yeah, I know. I probably shouldn't name a chapter 'Little Fuckers' but it makes me happy. I do love the little childrens, don't get me wrong. I even have one, and I assure you that he is not an asshole when we dine out. Or ever. He never has been. As a small, newly mobile human, on the rare occasion he would accidentally drop something on the floor of a restaurant, he would pick it up. Why? Because I taught him some basic fucking manners, that's why. I also told him to make sure his public behaviour reflects well upon me as a parent.

There was this one time however, when The Boy was about 10, that he ordered a cheeseburger off the kids menu and the waitress brought him an order of pancakes. My boy says to her, with a smart-assed grin and a heavy hint of sarcasm, "That's a funny looking cheeseburger." Ok, maybe that one time he was, but that sarcasm is genetic and he couldn't help it. I had to let it slide. The waitress was quick and witty and didn't miss a beat. She told him to mind his P's and Q's because if he hadn't realized it yet, she was the person handling his food. She left the rest up to his imagination. I left her a very nice tip.

Just because they're children doesn't mean they don't have to follow the rules of polite society the same as everyone else. Most importantly, remember to practice what you preach. I cannot tell you how many times adults force the please and thank you's and I never hear a single one out of their own mouths.

~~~~~

Table #67 let their child throw all the contents of the sugar caddy, salt and pepper shakers included, under the table and then left it. I wish they were my friends so I could unfriend them.

~~~

I got a cranky little puker at Table #24. It was pink. I may join him if I don't stop thinking about it.

~~~

I ask this as a personal favor:

Please do not let your children, or the children of your friends and family, smear their jelly laden lips upon the glass in any public place. We simply do not have the chemicals to accommodate this kind of disaster.

~~~

The best time for a parent to pick up the crackers and dry cereal from the area surrounding their table would be BEFORE their malnourished little crumb producers crush them into the carpet.

~~~

One of my regulars, who volunteers at the zoo, said that 2 children fell into the shark tank today. Several hours apart. It seems this happens quite often.

~~~

The hostess has a large basket containing only green crayons. We must be expecting loads of unimaginative children.

~~~

Table #40, a 4 top: Grandpa moved the highchair to pick up all the crap the kid dropped.

The mom says, "No dad...dad...dad no," then leans over to whisper, "That's what the tip is for."

The $2 tip.

I thanked him for his effort.

Wow mom. Way to teach the kid good manners and solid life skills.

~~~

A wild little guy grabbed a glass off my full tray. I yelled at him. He is lucky he didn't wear the contents.

~~~

At Table #72, there sat the absolute, most horrible little children I have ever waited on.

There were 11 of them and they were all under 5. Only 2 were not acting like sugar soaked squirrels frantically digging for nuts in a freak mid-winter thaw. Their mothers should be put on display in public stocks as punishment. It actually takes real effort to raise such poorly mannered, jerky kids. There was not a single other person in the entire restaurant that was not affected by their rude manners. There was screaming for no reason at all, crying, laying in the aisles, running all over, spilling shit, throwing things on the floor, cutting up of crayons and loads of other mass destruction. That I only scolded them a couple of times is a testament to the fact that I am even tempered.

They stayed for 2 long hours. What made me snap? One of the little assholes opened sugar packets (yes, plural) and dumped them out on a menu. Then he and his little asshole brother started driving their toy trucks around in it. Not a single adult said anything to them. Except me. Using my stern voice. You see what they've brought me to?! MY STERN VOICE.

Tragic.

~~~

My coworker Sh'Diamond's child is at Table #63. He is such a handsome little man. Very mannerly too!

~~~

I feel bad that the shrill screamer at Table #67 and the projectile vomiter at Table #65 made the woman at Table #63 request that her lunch be boxed up to go.

~~~

I have a yeller at Table #22. A very loud, enthusiastic yeller.

My condolences to whoever gets stuck with a screaming, yelling, obnoxious or otherwise volume gifted child in their section. It is not pleasant for anyone, especially the afflicted server. No one new will sit in the section while something like that is going on and people who are already there will move or leave. These things result in less money. Keep your ridiculously noisy children at home or remove them from the restaurant if they are suddenly seemingly possessed. If, after a couple minutes of trying to rein in this behaviour, you don't do exactly that, you are an asshole and so is your kid.

~~~

The boy at Table #65 is sure that macaroni and cheese will not make him puke, so he's going ahead with it.

~~~

At Table #32 sits a cross-eyed child with a yellow crayon jammed up his nose, oblivious. Ahhh, the sweet innocence of youth. Dora Lee said, "It's shoved up there so far, I'd be amazed if 'ola' could be read. 'Cray' was lost in his sinus cavity for sure!"

~~~

The cutie patootie 2 year old at Table #65 wouldn't tell me his name so I was guessing.

Me: "Is it Fred?"

Kid: "No."

Me: "Bill?"

Kid: "No."

Me: "Eric?"

Kid: "No."

Me: "Handsome?"

Kid: "Yes."

~~~

To all the little children who rearrange the jelly in the jelly caddies, and to the adults that don't have them put it to rights when they are done, eff you.

~~~

Table #71 let 3 of their children break crayons and rip straw paper into tiny pieces and then throw it on the floor, all while they ran around the dining room like coked up hyenas.

~~~

Table #70's three kids are rolling around on the floor in the aisle, right where I go in and out of the server aisle. I think they are trying to kill me.

~~~

The pre-teen kid at Table #25 has asked his mom several times if he could go to the bathroom. She is on her cell phone and cannot spare him a moment. I told him to go, she wouldn't even notice. He did. She didn't. Poor kid.

~~~

I had another puker at Table #62. It looked like he'd eaten copious amounts of oatmeal for breakfast.

~~~~~

Angel Woolery

16

Stuff I Thought You Should Know

I tell anyone who will listen all sorts of random stuff. My husband and my coworkers bear the brunt of it, followed closely by my Facebook friends and now, you. You're welcome.

~~~~~

It's only 10:50am and my tray arm is so tired.

~~~

I am in the middle of an enforced half hour break because I am scheduled more than 8 hours today and company policy demands it. I'm taking this free time to share my opinion of breaks. Breaks are for sissies and smokers. Breaks are a stupid, non-income producing waste of time which could be better spent spreading sunshine and serving pie. Breaks can suck it. That is all.

~~~

My polyester blend slacks are making my ass sweat.

~~~

There is a regular that comes in several times a week. He never says more than 10 words, sits in the same area and does not require much tending. He also does not tip. Ever.

There is a fabled dollar he left some years back, but no picture of said dollar can be produced.

We wait on him. We talk to him. We smile at him and make him welcome. He gets reasonably good service and we ignore his glaring lack of monetary etiquette.

How do I do this happily, week after week, month after month, knowing he is a seemingly TOTAL cheapskate?

Secretly I fantasize that he is filthy rich and has left us all in his will. Time will tell.

~~~

I work with a bunch of pretty mean girls. Oh wait. I mean pretty, mean girls.

~~~

Sure, I'll go get you a takeout box for your TINY-ASS bite of dessert! I'd rather you go ahead and eat it rather than adding to the plastic vortexes cluttering our lovely oceans. But you do you. Mother Earth can take care of herself.

And while I am on the subject, stop asking for a bag to carry your one take out box, you wasteful jerk.

~~~

I wonder at the science behind a little pre-work lovin' and the excellent gratuities that follow.

~~~

The Parsley Lobby must consist of thugs and ne'er do wells. I cannot imagine restaurants would use this pointless crap without coercion.

~~~

I have someone in my section that smells like pineapple, coconut and warm beaches. It is making me want a vacation.

~~~

I'm driving into work thinking what a drag it is. I don't want to work today. Then, I see lots of smoke covering a couple block area. I was kind of hoping it was work so I could go back home. No luck today. Sigh.

~~~

I have warmly welcomed Table #25.

~~~

I feel waitressing must have been in my family for millennia, as our women have evolved larger breasts. I believe it's for the sole purpose of counterbalancing the weight of a tray.

~~~

I am mentally and physically unprepared to serve food today. Groannnnn.

~~~

I am very concerned I may not be maintaining my smiley poker face at some of the tables I wait on.

~~~

I have a section full of adoring customers, ate a chicken strip and a warm yummy chocolate chip cookie that my sweet co-worker Kitty brought for me and I am in the freakin' zone.

~~~

I am off to work to welcome my customers in a formal, corporate approved manner while at the same time sounding natural and like I mean it. :(I'd rather hug them like usual! They like that!

Our company, as so many other companies have, has seen fit to supply us with a standard, lame-o corporate patter to use upon greeting customers and to use continuously throughout their dining experience, whether we know the customer or not. Because sounding like a "natural" robot is endearing, and invites people to feel like part of the family? I hardly think so. The only allowance made is that, if we know their names, we can use those instead.

I suck with names and I don't think calling my regulars by the nicknames we've cooked up for them would go over well. "How's it going Nemo?" "Your usual, Race Car Guy?" "Would you like a regular pop only to insist that it's diet pop and make me dump it out and refill it with the same kind I did to begin with, Crazy Swedish Woman? Because you do that nearly EVERY time." Now, I'd ignore this ridiculous edict but random customers are given surveys asking if we've done the stupid shit required of us. They don't know that we get in trouble if we don't do each step exactly. For instance, if the survey says, 'Did your server offer you two specific beverage choices?' and they say, "No" it counts against our score. It does not leave room for the customer to add 'My server had my beverage waiting for me at my favorite booth before my feet even crossed the threshold.' The customers do not know that too many violations can lead to dismissal. In some fields, anything less than the customer answering each question with "Excellent" ends with the employee having their pay reduced quite substantially until better surveys are turned in.

While I feel customer feedback is a valid form of accountability, I think there definitely need to be more relaxed questions. I, personally, as a customer refuse to fill these things out. If I did, I'd lie. I do not go places for a tight corporate feel. I return to establishments that make me welcome. This sort of crap squashes individuality. It can make an uncomfortable experience for the customer by not allowing the employee to assess the situation and use the appropriate communication for the circumstances. For example: The hosts at one of the places where my husband and I like to eat make small talk with us all the way to our table. I don't want to small talk with someone who does not actually give two shits about how I respond. Bring me to my table and give me a menu young host person. That is all I require of you.

Secret Shoppers are also on the prowl. These are people hired by a company to come in with a set of questions to be filled out after their visit. It is a more formal system for making sure employees are blindly following corporate policy. Depending on the business they are shopping, they could be compensated for their meal or a purchased item of clothing or paid cash. Not a bad idea on the whole if the shoppers were pre-screened to make sure they were sane and able to pay attention to details. I've seen some strange shop reports that make me wonder if they'd been hitting the crack pipe before coming in to pay attention to said small details.

I feel that I have properly ranted about this subject and I may now move on.

~~~

I speak in a full on whine, "Why is it only half past 1:00? Whhhyyyy? It's sooooo slow."

Please entertain me. Text. Send naked pictures. Anything!! Please!!

~~~

I am bonding with Table #52. They "get" me and think I'm hilarious. I <3 u Table #52. I really do.

~~~

My H.R. guy had the pleasure of making my acquaintance today. Sadly, he was just in to have a bite and not because I was the subject of a potentially scandalous lawsuit.

~~~

I am saltier than a bag of chips.

~~~

I'm bored, stuck at work and I can taste perfume.

~~~

It no longer amuses me to punch a clock.

~~~

I wonder how many hours of my life have been spent pushing in chairs and returning salt and pepper shakers to their caddies.

~~~

Work is simply a distraction from life, creation and the pursuit of happiness. Work can suck it.

~~~

I am hot.

So hot.

Tasting rather salty and experiencing minor chafing.

~~~

My husband does not find my waitress clothes attractive.

~~~

I am becoming a billionaire one painful little dollar at a time.

~~~

I was violently attacked by the frosting bottle and ended up coated in it from apron to toe.

~~~

Immaverysweatywaitress.

~~~

My tray arm is so tired by the time Friday comes around.

~~~

Someone aimed an infrared meat thermometer at me today. It turns out I am a steamy hot 94 degrees.

~~~

It's really hard to stay riled up with Peaches & Herb's dulcet tones cascading from the work stereo.

~~~

Boob sweat. It comes with the job. Lots of it.

*****

17

Injuries to My Person and My Psyche

A coworker once told me that the definition of stress was long periods of boredom interrupted by short periods of terror. That pretty much sums up waitressing.

I should get hazard pay. This job is injurious in all kinds of unmentionable ways and I am just talking day to day. I won't even mention the long-term damage to my body and soul. That is a whole 'nother book.

~~~~~

Table #61 smells like the carpet deodorizer I used when I lived in Japan.

You know that perfumey crap you sprinkle before you vacuum? I could have gone my whole life without ever smelling that again. Now, I get to breathe it in every week. I could develop the room deodorizing equivalent of popcorn lung if I am not careful.

~~~

I have discovered some moderately painful bruising on my person as a result of ice machine shenanigans. I may need Rose to stay late tomorrow should it become too difficult to carry on in such a state.

*The ice machine was broken, empty and being fixed. The repairman was nowhere in sight. The machine was looking at Rose and I in an inviting, come hither way. What were we to do? We scampered over before anyone could catch us and I half dove, half climbed inside, left my legs sticking out, as if the machine was trying to gobble me whole, and Rose snapped a photo.

I sustained minor injuries but it was all worth it.

~~~

I cry about once a year, while I am working, due to waitress related stress. It usually happens directly after I am forced to yell at someone for their boneheaded stupidity that caused me my waitress stress. Today was not the day.

~~~

Table #52 lifted up his shirt to look at his belly.

~~~

A nice lady from Table #70 tipped me and then went out to her car and brought me back a bag that held a bunch of candy and a couple of religious tracts. I feel bad that I can't eat it.

Jesus candy makes me very suspicious.

~~~

My stupid backup hairspray bottle split stream like man pee. It very nearly got me in the eye thus blinding me and rendering me incapable of working today.

~~~

Table #40 asked me again if I'd spoken to his dead wife recently.

She died a few months ago. He is heartbroken and he deals with it by trying to make light of it. I finally had to ask him to stop because it makes me feel so bad when he says it.

~~~

I felt the wrath of the Waitressing Gods today. Brutal. No doubt it was delivered unto me for earlier sass.

#busyashell

~~~

One of my first tables today had the jelly caddy dumped out and was enthusiastically rearranging. The universe is toying with me.

~~~

We were crazy busy, so I was going the speed of light when I hit the pantry floor with my inappropriate, slidey bottomed work shoes. Of course, I slipped and fell at that same speed, and came to a bone-jarring stop. An undignified heap of frazzled waitress, dirty plates and a large, impending chiropractor bill was all that remained. Pitiful.

~~~

I inadvertently gave our prep guy Emilio an eyeful when I squatted down and bent over to retrieve something from underneath a deep shelf. My low riding pants decided to slide down and my short shirttails shimmied up to reveal the top part of my wintry white, middle-aged badunkadunk and the black thong that attempted and failed miserably to provide adequate coverage. Now he keeps smiling at me.

~~~

I consider having to work with people who are wearing cologne or perfume a hostile work environment.

I am not a fan of perfume. Occasionally I will catch a gentle whiff of something pleasant that ever so softly tickles my senses. Anything more than that I find revolting. That said, food and perfume do not mix. I have had customers and coworkers absolutely doused in department store stank. It's horrible. It physically cuts off my air and I have to stand back from the table so I can breathe. Anyone working or dining in a restaurant should be banned from wearing it. People are there to taste the food, not some noxious, bottled chemical masquerading as a bouquet of pleasantries. Take a nice hot shower and you will smell divine.

~~~

I made coffee too hard at work today. I still have grounds in my hair. I'm trying to pick them off my scalp before I shower so they don't end up brewing in the steamy heat.

~~~

While carrying a tray crammed full of water glasses, I realized it was too heavy. By the time I arrived at the first table, it was too late. My right hand was holding something else and was of no use to me. My left hand started trembling and the tray started rocking. That sucker was going over and it was me or them. I had a split second to decide. I used the remaining strength in my tray arm and tipped it toward myself. Hundreds of tiny ice cubes applauded my selfless act as they chased a good gallon of water down the pristine white of my new work clothes. I was wet, cold, transparently clad and stuck at work for an eternity. Next time I don't know if I'm going to be willing to take the hit.

~~~

I have worked so many hours this week that my right butt cheek is starting to cramp up.

~~~

I will no doubt roll my eyes too hard someday and cause myself an injury.

~~~

The dishwasher, affectionate in her own way, called me a fat ass. I wonder if Work Comp covers lost hours due to hurt feelings?

~~~

I hope that if I am ever super old and sporting a mustache, that someone will kindly take me to get it waxed off.

So many of my older women customer have wild, disturbingly long, dark, wiry facial hair. Mustaches, beards, random eyebrows, forests growing out of their nostrils, you name it. My German heritage is making itself known as well, I'm not judging. I'd appreciate it if my friends or family members would take me to have them professionally removed if there ever comes a time that my eyesight is too poor to see them, my hands shake too hard to pull them or if I am just batshit crazy enough to not care. I am telling you now. I care. Help Angel.

~~~

I hate it when I have found a second to run to the bathroom, I get all zipped up and proper again and go back to work only to discover that my undies are askew and are going to have to stay that way. For hours.

#pantydance #wigglewigglewigglewigglewiggle

~~~

I am worried that if my endlessly tense right butt cheek ever decides to charlie horse, it will be bad. Very, very bad.

~~~

While working in a pizza place, I answered the phone for a takeout order. The guy asked me what ingredients we had. I rattled them all off. He asked me to tell him a second time. I did, thinking I'd gone too fast. Then he asked me to tell him again. I thought it was weird and maybe he was dumb, so I read them slower. About halfway through, I heard his breathing quicken and get heavy. I was a little late to the party I guess. I hung up on him. Sick fucker. If green peppers and anchovies float your boat buddy, more power to you, but I am not getting paid 2.99 a minute to talk you through.

~~~

That shift was so stupid long that I feel like a Barbie doll that some wicked little girl kept trying to separate the joints of. It hurts.

~~~

I'm at work and it's still dark out. I am suffering through a moment of 'grown up' and I do not like it. Not one little bit.

~~~

I had a customer make me sing *Happy Birthday* despite my strong recommendation to the contrary. I did it, but her ears may never be the same. Serves her right.

~~~

I am limping a little, but I dished out the food with enthusiasm!! What's a little pain?

~~~

I threw my (insert many expletives) back out at work. Only generously applied Hot/Cold patches saw me through a ten-hour, busy as hell day, seemingly uncrippled.

Is this what old feels like? I realized I was approaching old when I caught a glimpse of my chunky, thong bedecked ass, crowned with the above mentioned medicated patches as I walked half naked into the bathroom at home. Not attractive. A frightening peek into my future should I keep waitressing.

~~~

I almost made it out of the dining room with that party
sized tray of dirty dishes propped on my little shoulder. Then
the universe intervened, thinking it would be more fun if I
slipped for no apparent reason, and sent the contents of that
party sized tray of dirty dishes crashing loudly to the floor.
When the glass shards, silverware, used food and waitress
dust settled, I looked up to assess the damage. My whole, full
section was looking at me with a mixture of horror and
sympathy. That's when I started to cry.

~~~

The chocolate milk of a stranger soaking through the back
of my pant leg, chilling my calf, grosses me out.

~~~

There is a strange smell lingering over my section like gas
fumes in heavy traffic on a humid 1970's summer day. It took
hours but I've finally identified it: hand sanitizer and
department store cologne.

~~~

I have such a work shoe problem that I am gimpy when I
stand up to walk for at least a day or two after I work. My feet
feel like someone has been punching the bottoms. My bunion
has a bruise, and my bruise has a blister. My husband's
pocketbook is now lighter because I purchased a $129 pair of
slip resistant Danskos. Cross your fingers, because if these
don't work I will have to rely solely upon the money I make
as a nude art model.

~~~

I have to ask strangers repeatedly if I can warm their pie. This is no doubt having a significant effect upon me in ways I cannot yet fathom.

~~~

After having climbed up on a shelf, using the coffee machine as my brace and overextending my 5' frame to reach an even higher shelf, I felt my tummy getting warm. I paid it no mind as I was exerting myself and one is bound to get a little warm when exerting, right?

That warm feeling was the journey that the boiling hot tea water made as it soaked through my apron, skirt, shirt and nylons as I leaned unwittingly against the boiling hot water spigot. Don't worry, after it gently passed through the outer layers of my clothing, I discovered it with a yelp and pulled it off my flesh before it could sear through my guts. I am unscarred.

Physically, anyways.

~~~

My right butt cheek is in no danger of cramping up thanks to Rose's healing touch.

There is nothing wrong with a mid-shift butt massage by a caring coworker. Don't judge.

~~~

My olfactory nerves are burnt out after the repetitive inhaling of especially pungent old people smell.

~~~

The bad news: I found out my exact mental snapping point at work today - 30 customers spread out over 15 tables all at one time.

The good news: Crying at work only happens once a year or so. I'm golden for about 364 more days.

*****

18

All in a Day's Work

Table #43 only sat there for a minute or two before he
disappeared. Rose and I assumed he went to the bathroom.
After about a half hour of wondering what the poor guy had
eaten to keep him in the potty so long, we figured he must
have died. There was much discussion about the possibility
of finding him splayed on the bathroom floor and how no
one had actually ever died while in the restaurant so far and
how it seemed completely possible that it had finally
happened. We knew it was only a matter of time.

Rose was brave enough to go look. Whew! No dead body.
He must've gone out the front door when we weren't looking.

~~~

It seems we have some cleptos at Table #68, with a
creamer dish fetish. This is the 3rd time it has gone missing.

~~~

A bunch of cops were surrounding a table of regulars for a goodly amount of time. It was driving me wild not knowing what was going on! When all was said and done, I found out that a customer thought they'd recognized one of the guys as being featured on the TV show America's Most Wanted. It turns out he wasn't, thank goodness! He's a damn good tipper and cute to boot!

I'd hate to lose him to Federal Prison.

~~~

I'm lucky to have one of the few jobs where I can walk around with whipped cream on my boob and nobody even bats a lash.

~~~

The 3 grown adults at Table #69 have their IPads flipped open, propped at a comfortable angle and are virtual farming together.

~~~

I was seating a dude at Table #62. As I set the menu down, he blows on past me and says, "I have to go to the can, but I'll have coffee."

#classy

~~~

The Gods of Waitressing desire my continued service and bestowed upon me a 100% on my recent Secret Shop. YAY! This means I will not be fired. Yet.

~~~

I had the personal joy of waiting on Ballscratcher and his grandma. My day can only improve. Right?

Overall they are nice people. Except for the occasional, horrible lapse in manners and the fact that they can be taxing to the raw nerves of a busy waitress. One of the things they enjoy is asking about the calorie content in pie while we are in the middle of a frazzling lunch rush. They require about 10 minutes and the book of nutritional information. Seriously, if one is concerned about calorie content in ANY way, don't eat fucking pie. Yeah, I said it. There is no piece of pie or cake that we have that does not fall into the 500-1200 calorie range. We waitresses have turned this harassing duty over to the managers as there may be violence done if left in the hands of any of us.

Maybe not today. Maybe not next time. But it could happen.

~~~

I walked into work to the news that Rose and I would be taking the large funeral party.

We are the most somber. Only proper.

~~~

Table #54: "I'm sorry. I'm going to be a pain in the butt today."

Me: "That's ok. You are every time. I'm used to it."

Ok, I didn't say it but I thought it really loud.

~~~

I was telling Table #25 about someone I used to deliver pizzas to, a woman who smoked so much that her white, 3-legged poodle was tobacco stained.

Table #25 said I could write a book.

What a great idea!!

~~~

Table #62: "I'll have the Alabaster Tuna Melt."

~~~

Table #63 said, "My eggs are bland. I don't even know what would make an egg bland."

Me: "Unimaginative chickens?"

I laughed. He did not.

~~~

Overheard at Table #74: "Thank God for Dick Cheney for making us safer."

~~~

I let the old lady at Table #42 feel my impressive deltoid.

~~~

Table #12. White guy, black girl. Possibly on a date. Probably special needs. They are making me happy.

Me to woman: "Corn bread or Focaccia?"

Woman: "Neither one."

Guy to woman: "Don't your people like corn bread?"

Omg.

~~~

A stranger walked through the front door and told me he needed to see my equipment because a new "cheesemelter" was going to be installed. I have met my match. He left me speechless with a mind full of possibilities.

~~~

Co-worker: "I have to tell you something. You're going to laugh your ass off, but you'll look funny running around without your ass."

Me: "My assless chaps will fit better though."

~~~

Rose and I hadn't seen a sweet married couple that came in regularly in quite a while. We were very worried, so one day after work we drove around to several assisted living buildings in the area until we found them, alive and well. They were very surprised to see us. It seems they'd been in often and we just hadn't asked the right coworkers about them.

~~~

At Table #66 sits the naughty cream dish stealers. They are sad. I brought them a soup cup and it does not match their set. Muahahaha!

~~~

Overheard at Table #43, and said with absolute authority:

"The best place to eat a Popsicle? Bathtub!"

~~~

Note to self: Don't joke with customers about shrinkage no matter how funny I think it is.

~~~

I have not seen a rubber wearing man in ages! Thank you Table #51 for bringing me joy.

Since my co-worker Rose is English, I sometimes, as a courtesy, speak her language. It helps her not miss her mates from across the pond so much.

~~~

I curtsied to Table #61. They didn't bat a lash.

~~~

I had the singular pleasure of waiting on Ballscratcher today. He hasn't willingly spoken to me in 5 years. Today was my lucky day. I said something to him that set off a torrent of excited chatter. He went on for ten minutes and I was having a slight bit more affinity for him when he started cleaning under his fingernails. Then, all I could think was: There must be copious amounts of ball sweat and/or fromunda cheese on his fingers. Ish.

~~~

Table #33 dude sounds like a hormonal teenaged girl. It's not pretty.

I put "whiny bitch" very low on my list of attractive man traits.

~~~

I got a surprise job review today. Despite my certainty the term "H.R. Time Bomb" would be brought into play, it turned out I am an excellent employee with a good work ethic. I will try harder.

~~~

I spilled a whole lot of dressing in the middle of the server aisle floor.

Rose said to me, "You losing your sauce is like a truck losing its load."

#theycallmeangelsauce

~~~

My ability to not giggle in the face of absurdity is being sorely tested by Table #50. I will paint you a word picture: A mid-50ish woman, with unnaturally red hair bordering on orange and a large bald spot. Oh wait, not a bald spot, just 1 1/2 inch long gray roots. Long, old, crusty looking fake nails. Tattoo on top of her hand. Red shirt and white sweat pants with red, fuzzy socks. Black lace-up high heels. Smells as if she's been rolling in Tide.

~~~

I think I am in the midst of a harsh karmic rebalance.

An icky dude felt the need to try to charm me with his annoying wit. Some other weirdo stared at my boobs without even bothering to pretend he wasn't, and I think my tooth is cracked. I must've done something superbad.

~~~

I have butter up in my shirtsleeve. Sigh. How??

~~~

I was in the dining room chuckling to myself. I looked up and two separate tables are giving me the eye. Busted. Oops.

~~~

My "Service Industry Smile" is slipping and it's not even 3:00 yet.

~~~

OMFG. The creamer dish thieves have stolen the 4 oz ramekin. Seriously? We have secured management approval to place their creamers directly on the table and have a talk with them should they question the lack of cream cozies in the future.

~~~

Table #53 is looking at me like I'm super weird. This is indicative of a huge tip. I am excited.

~~~

The downside: Ballscratcher was picking his nose while he talked to me.

The upside: He was actually talking to me.

~~~

Wig woman is busting my balls today.

She has the most atrociously fitting wig I have ever seen. Someone once likened her appearance to the Hawaiian Punch guy. No lie, the resemblance is uncanny. She is a cranky nightmare until she eats. Then, she is as sweet as pie, but her wig still doesn't fit any better.

~~~

Oooo! I sold one of my poetry books to one of my most favorite regulars. Super jazzed! I hope he likes it.

He is super nice and I love it when he comes in. He always has great stories and kind words. I published a poetry book called 'The Taste of Innocence'. It is my first book. (Available on Amazon!) Some parts are a little steamy. I wasn't going to tell my customers I was published because I am a little shy about it, but I am a chatty gal and he showed genuine interest.

Eeek!! He's reading it while he sits here. *bites nails* I hope he's reading a tame one.

Crap. He is still reading. I'm guessing the whole thing because it's gone on so long. *deep breaths* (Me, not him.)

I couldn't take it anymore and I could see he was at the end and was flipping back through it so I snuck up to his table and said, "Well, you haven't demanded your money back yet."

He says, "Wow" and then lists three of his favorites, and that I have gotten to the line and crossed over it, and that it is really, really good and …then I don't remember the rest in my glee. He was very complimentary and I am much relieved! *spinning in happy circles*!!

One of my managers (who does not like poetry yet because he's never read any of mine) relayed to me, that when the customer that bought my book was leaving, he said to him, "I hope it doesn't make you soft!" The guffaws that escaped Dora Lee and I could likely be heard outside. I can only imagine what the customer was thinking. Geez! Our manager explained, amidst our booming laughter, that he was referring to the man's heart. Ha!

~~~

The creamer dish thieves are in my section. They must know we've caught on to their shenanigans because the guy specifically ordered 1 cream and completely wrecked our fun.

~~~

We are in the middle of the bar rush and I have a huge, full party tray on my left shoulder. I'm going fast as I round the corner of the atrium to deliver Table #13's food only to be brought to an immediate halt. Surrounding Table #13 are 6-8 cops with their guns drawn. I made eye contact with the one closest to me when he turned to assess if I were a threat or not. "I just want to drop off the food," I say to him with my eyes. He shook his head "no". Sigh. I had to bring it back to the kitchen window and explain to the cooks why it was coming back. Never a good thing.

I am happy to report that the situation was handled in under 5 minutes and my people got their food. It turns out one of the customers had a laser pointer and someone at the front of the restaurant saw it, thought it was the scope light on a gun and called the police.

~~~

I am trying real hard not to eff up Table #22's dining experience. Something ALWAYS goes wrong for them. It's just the way of it.

~~~

Table #76 woman: "What's good today? Last time, the crepes were horrible!"

Me: "Not the crepes?"

~~~

Woot! I got a sleeper. The 30ish year old woman at Table #25 is fast asleep, sitting up, her head resting forward upon her ample bosom.

~~~

One of the ladies at Table #74 is looking at me in such a bizarre way that I wouldn't be surprised if her face unhinged and a small alien popped out to ask for more pancakes. I'm a little creeped out.

~~~

Ballscratcher addressed me by name and thanked me. There may be hope for humanity.

~~~

Table #35 comes toward me waving a $5. "Can you give this to Angel? Oh! You are Angel!"

Both of my hands were full so I held out the tray so she could put it on there.

Table #35, heading for my left breast pocket: "I'll just tuck it in here."

Uhm, ok.

Table #35, making solid boob contact with the back of her hand several times while tucking: "It's ok, I'm a nurse."

Hilarious!

~~~

This woman's pants are so far up the crack of her ass it looks like a vacuum-packed chunk of pork loin. She may need the Jaws of Life to extract them.

~~~

Me: "How are you today?"

Table #34: "Tired."

Me: "I'll wake you up."

Table #34: "Don't hurt me."

Me: "I'll try not to."

~~~

The creamer dish thieves stole the cracked creamer dish that we reserve solely for their use. They are now cut off. No dish will ever cradle their cream again.

~~~

A coworker was explaining how she didn't need a man.

Coworker: "Men are a pain in the ass."

Me: "Then you're not doing it right."

~~~

I lost my nametag. What will people call me now? Ma'am?

~~~

A customer comes wandering toward me with a menu in hand.

Customer: "I'd like to sit in your section today."

Me: I gesture toward 2 tables and 11 open booths. 2 are occupied, 1 is dirty. This leaves 10 clean, ready to use ones. "This is my section."

Customer points to a table: "I'll take that one."

Me: "The dirty one?"

Customer: "Yes."

~~~

I do not know how I am supposed to get all my communicating done when there are all these "employer requirements".

~~~

I am spreading happiness one slice of pie at a time.

~~~

I approached a new customer for a drink order. She flipped a quarter on the table. Enticement?

~~~

I wonder how many plates of food my left boob has dipped into in my many years of waitressing. The number must be staggering!

~~~

My waitress uniform looks like an unwilling participant in a food fight.

~~~

I wish people would stop looking at me with their heads tipped sideways, wearing a perplexed expression. It makes me self-conscious.

~~~

I'm probably going to freebase some coffee at work today.

~~~

In the midst of a nationwide egg recall...

Woman at table #58, of her Eggs Benedict: "Can I get the eggs scrambled instead of basted?"

Me: "Sure."

Man at table #58: "She's worried they won't be cooked enough and that they aren't safe."

Me: "We haven't killed anyone yet."

Stop watching the news people! It only causes unnecessary anxiety.

~~~

I know it's hot when even the pie is sweaty.

~~~

My sass will surely provoke the wrath of the pie gods.

~~~

The creamer dish thieves, lacking a creamer dish to satisfy their sticky fingers, stole a small plate. I am almost certain of it.

~~~

I am on my 2nd eye roll, 1st heavy sigh, 14th witty comment, and madly cackled moments ago. Only 5 1/2 hours left.

~~~

Table #68 guy: "I'll have the Craps."

I brought him Crepes instead. He didn't notice the difference.

~~~

More butter Table #50? Really? Wouldn't it be quicker to just spread it on your ass?

~~~

I am taunting the Gods of Waitressing today by wearing a brand new white blouse. They will no doubt retaliate. Something will end up berried!

~~~

I know the newly enforced cell phone policy at work was not intended for me.

~~~

There was a bomb threat at the drugstore next to my J.O.B. today. The cops taped off most of our parking lot and had all of our customers sit in the rear half of the restaurant to avoid possible injury. I am not one to let some whack-job with a telephone and too much time on their hands ruin my sales. For my customers, I suggested they order their dessert first. Just in case.

~~~

Cripes!! The old people are hostile today!

~~~

Not having the items on the menu available for the guests is very frustrating. When it happens repeatedly due to negligence on the part of our new, temporary manager, Dora Lee gets hulkish.

For about the 10th time in two weeks Dora Lee sold a pot pie at lunchtime only to be told that we were out, again. Pot pies take a long time to bake and should be one of the first things done in the morning.

Manager, looking sheepish: "We don't have any made yet. Sorry."

Dora Lee yells at her, "There are no pot pies AGAIN? Unfuckingbelieveable."

I think from that point forward, there were pot pies. Dora Lee meant business.

~~~

I find nothing quite as ooky as leaning over to wipe a table and finding my knee resting in a recently vacated, disturbingly warm, ass spot.

~~~

I want to know, if a woman orders strawberry creeps, what should I bring her?

~~~

I've dipped my right boob in berry sauce twice now and it's not even lunch yet.

~~~

Table #64 showed me his new false teeth. Out of his mouth.

~~~

The old lady at Table #33 is missing a shoe.

~~~

A party of 8 sat at Table #70, a large conference table with big squishy chairs. They hadn't been there 10 seconds before they got my waitress feathers all in a kerfuffle. First, they wanted more room so asked for the furniture to be moved away from the wall. This required not only moving all 8 big squishy chairs and the heavy table, but 4 other tables and 10 other chairs so that there would still be an aisle to walk through after rearranging to make them happy with the seating. They did not even notice the hassle that the request caused. Second, three of them ordered hot water with lemon. You know how I feel about hot water drinkers.

When they ordered their food, one of the men requested his cornbread be "so hot he could not touch it." I was more than happy to oblige for this one. I put his bread in the microwave for two minutes instead of the customary twenty seconds. I brought it out very proud of myself. He touched it with the back of his hand and announced that it was not nearly hot enough. WHAT? Fine. I returned it to the microwave for two more minutes and went back out into the dining room to give my other customers a little attention.

Dora Lee was the first one back into the server aisle, where she was greeted with a huge plume of smoke rolling out of the microwave. Thinking the microwave was ablaze, she hollers, "What should I do?" and simultaneously opens the door with one hand while ducking and moving forward in one motion. I believe her military training put her into immediate full combat mode. It was beautiful! The cooks stood staring through the food window with their arms crossed over their chests, shaking their heads and judging my cooking abilities. Dammit! Amidst our loud, amused cackling, I put another piece in for 3 minutes. That seemed reasonable since a combined total of 4 minutes ended in tragedy. I went back out the dining room. Upon my return I found smoke billowing out as hellfire once again visited an innocent piece of corn bread. It hadn't even completed its 3 minute cycle. Holy crap! What is in this cornbread? I put the third piece in for the original 2 minutes.

I went out to the table to let the customer know what taking so long. I said to him straight faced, "It seems that at 2 ½ minutes cornbread ignites." His companions started hooting with laughter and teasing him for being so picky.

I saved the blackened objects of our amusement so that I could take a picture to share with my friends. One of the gals from that table stuck her head into the back to ask if I still had it so that she could take a photo of it. I posed with the picky man and the charred bread for a little photo documentation and a good time was had by all.

A perfect end to a crappy situation.

The horrible smell lingered for days. Everyone suffered and I will never live it down.

~~~

The creamer dish thieves were in today. They were witness to a thorough waitress ass kicking. Good lord was it busy! On their way out, the wife gave me a random, earnest hug of support for my overworked waitress self. It was very sweet.

*****

Angel Woolery

156

The End

I was hoping to end this book with news of my wildly successful career as a trapeze artist in a travelling circus, or maybe friend to a celebrity who allowed me to live in their pool house simply because I am an amusing guest who doesn't eat too much, but no. To my dismay, neither has happened and I still find myself punching a dumb waitress clock. By the time I publish, I imagine I will have to quit to save myself the inevitability of getting fired. Not because I've said anything that could be legal grounds for termination, but because clearly, I don't want to be a waitress anymore and my boss is a kind, loving person. I would expect her to put me out of my misery.

I also have a job interview in a few days.

Angel Woolery

About the Author

Encouraged by her mother after expressing a desire to serve customers, Angel started waitressing in her family's restaurant when she was just 8 years old. She also started writing about the same time. It seems fitting that the two now join together.

Angel Woolery's published works include:

The Taste of Innocence – A Book of Poetry

and as a contributing author in:

Behind The Veil
On The Verge
Into The Abyss

All available on Amazon.com.

Angel would love to hear from on you on the web:

Facebook Page: Angel Woolery – Writer
Facebook Page: Angel Woolery – Poet